P9-CDM-848

HERE'S JOHNNY!

HERE'S JOHNNY!

Ed McMahon

RUTLEDGE HILL PRESS®
Nashville, Tennessee
A Division of Thomas Nelson Publishers
www.ThomasNelson.com

Published by Rutledge Hill Press, a Division of Thomas Nelson, Inc., P.O. Box 141000, Nashville, Tennessee, 37214.

Rutledge Hill Press books may be purchased in bulk for educational, business, fund-raising, or sales promotional use. For information, please e-mail SpecialMarkets@ThomasNelson.com.

Library of Congress Cataloging-in-Publication Data

McMahon, Ed.

Here's Johnny! : my memories of Johnny Carson, the Tonight show, and 46 years of friendship /Ed McMahon.

p. cm.

ISBN 1-4016-0236-3 (hardcover)

1. Carson, Johnny, 1925–2005 2. McMahon, Ed. 3. Television personalities—United States—Biography. 4. Tonight show (Television program) I. Title.

PN1992.4.C28M36 2005

791.4502'8'092—dc22

2005019304

Printed in the United States of America

05 06 07 08 09 — 9 8 7 6 5 4 3 2 1

Only one possible dedication:

To Johnny

Contents

CONTENTS

HERE'S JOHNNY!

warmup

And Hilarity Ensues

Almost five thousand times, Johnny Carson walked through those colored curtains after I had taken a considerable amount of time to say two words: "Heeeeere's Johnny!" Almost five thousand times he walked out to the sound of a song he had helped to write, in a unique style that defined debonair, and with a grin that brought to mind the cutest kid in detention, to show millions of Americans the happiest way to end the day.

Ever since Johnny Carson's final passage through those curtains on May 22, 1992, so many sweet bits of all those shows have been rerunning in my mental VCR—my "Very Cherished Remembrances." I awaken in the middle of the night and hear myself saying to Aunt Blabby, "*I haven't seen you in a long time.*"

Globe Photos, Inc.

Supplied by NBC/Globe Photos, Inc.

And I hear Aunt Blabby reply, "*You haven't seen your shoes in a long time either.*"

And I hear Johnny as Mister Rogers merrily telling all the boys in the neighborhood what to do to all the girls as he merrily sings:

> *It's a go-to-bed day in the neighborhood,*
> *A day to kiss any cute neighbor who would . . .*

And I see a python slipping between Johnny's legs while the look on his face seems to say he's wondering if the snake has mistaken him for a tree or is checking to see if his fly is closed.

And I hear Carnac the Magnificent say that the question for "These are a few of my favorite things" was "*What do you say to a doctor wearing rubber gloves?*" and the question for "Chicken Teriyaki" was "*What is the name of the last surviving kamikaze pilot?*" And the question for "All systems go" was "*What happens if you take a Sinutab, a Maalox, and a Feen-a-Mint?*"

NBC/Globe Photos, Inc.

Associated Press, Douglas C. Pizac

And I see myself interviewing Johnny as Shirley Temple after she has become a candidate for congress and I am fighting back laughter, for "Shirley" has just sung:

> *On the Good Ship Lollipop,*
> *Where the jollies never stop.*

And I see—and I hear—the greatest smorgasbord of entertainment in the history of American show business.

"Smorgasbord, Ed?" I can hear Johnny saying now. *"Sometimes a Spam sandwich too."* And once in a while, a ptomaine tamale.

"*But Johnny,*" I reply, "*absolutely everyone has said that your show was the best thing that ever happened to TV.*"

"*They're forgetting* Romper Room."

After reading inflated copy for a new NBC sitcom, Johnny used to say with a roll of his blue eyes, "And hilarity ensues." He would read something like:

About to delight you on Wednesdays at nine is a new show called *Foot and Mouth.* Tired of the singles scene on Iwo Jima, nine cool young podiatrists move to a loony loft in Greenwich Village, hoping to start with feet and move up. And hilarity ensues.

And right after that hilarity, Wednesdays at nine thirty, is *Dear Darwin.* Unable to find an apartment, Louella moves into the Bronx Zoo where she falls head over heels for a chimpanzee who's been head over heels a lot too. But Louella does have a problem, and not just that the chimp is two feet shorter and not Methodist. Can she take him home to her mother as her boyfriend or should her story be that he's just a pet? *Dear Darwin* will have you going both ape and bananas. In a show that will quickly become your favorite inter-species romp, a lovable lunatic looks for her place in both New York and evolution. And hilarity ensues.

"And hilarity ensues." But only in my misty mind.

He was a shy and private man, who once said to me, "I'm good with ten million, lousy with ten." He ran from tributes faster than he ran on the tennis court, faster than he ran from a growling baby leopard and jumped into my arms when I showed that a good second banana knows how to catch the star. Of course, for every other moment in our thirty years on *The Tonight Show,* Johnny Carson carried me.

He was a man who could make the sharpest ad libs, recover from the worst jokes, and do the longest comic double takes; but one night in his dressing room, while smoking what must have been his hundredth unfiltered cigarette of the day, he said, "Ed, I just don't know how to take compliments."

"You've gotten some of those, have you?" I said.

"Yeah, one last week from a UPS guy, but he must've thought I was Dick Clark."

We were able to joke about almost anything, but Johnny was serious now. He simply did not know how to respond to the legions of people who knew he was America's classiest entertainer.

"*Legions, Ed?*" I hear him saying. *"Is that the American or the French Foreign?"*

"*Johnny, I just meant that an awful lot of people love you and also know you're a very nice guy.*"

"I wish my first three wives had been among them."

"*But not Alex,*" I hear myself saying.

"No, I finally got it right."

"*And so did I with Pam.*"

"We were slow learners, weren't we, Ed?"

one

The Book of the Century

"Johnny," I said a few months before he died, "we've had so many wonderful memories, both on and off the show, that nobody knows about."

"We'd better keep it that way," he said, "especially that night at Jilly's when those two nutty . . . Of course, we didn't *do* anything."

"No, not that memory, but all the others. I'd love to share them with everyone in a book."

"Well, you're the only one to do it," he said. "And you can do it anytime in the next century."

"But so many people . . ."

Our childhood photos reveal that from middy blouses to blue suits, both Johnny and I avoided maturity along the way.

Nate Cutler/Globe Photos, Inc.

"Ed, write *A Boy's Life of Wayne Newton* first. Or *The Wit and Wisdom of Fats Domino.* Or the story of the Lincoln Tunnel: *For Whom the Tolls.* Or . . ."

"Stop!" I said, laughing hard. "Johnny, there are so many worthless books being published."

"And you want to write another one? Hey, how about writing *The Joy of Zinc* for all the people who find romance in minerals?"

"Seriously, Johnny," I said, "every day a dozen people ask me, 'What's Johnny Carson really like?'"

"The same dozen? Well, just tell them the truth. I'm an easy-going sociopath whose hobbies are bungee jumping, collecting swimsuit pictures of Jack LaLanne, and doing Zen meditation with P. Diddy. We pray for a new name for him."

Too Soon

My heart breaks to think that I do not have to wait until the year 2100 to write my memories of Johnny Carson. At a few minutes after seven o'clock on the morning of January 23, 2005, the telephone rang in my Beverly Hills house. My wife, Pam, answered it and her hand fell to her heart. As the blood drained from her face, she silently handed the phone to me. I didn't need Sherlock Holmes to know what had happened.

"Johnny," I said.

Pam's look said it all. In dismay, I took the phone.

"Ed," said Johnny's nephew, Jeff Sotzing, "Johnny just died."

"Oh, no, *no*."

"You're my first call. He would have wanted me to call you first. I know how much you two meant to each other."

Being at a loss for words isn't my style, but it was then.

"Jeff . . . I . . . I don't know what to say."

"You don't have to."

"I'm reeling now. Let me call you back."

Then I started to cry—the first tears that Pam ever saw me shed.

The following day, I just lay in bed, watching all the tributes to Johnny, crying one minute, laughing the next. It was a style of mourning you don't often see.

"Ed," I can hear Johnny saying, *"you needed a grief counselor. Or maybe one for volleyball."*

In the following weeks, I went on many radio and TV shows, on each of them paying tribute to Johnny. And one day, his widow, Alexis, called.

"Ed," she said, "I've seen everything you've done. You've been magnificent."

"Johnny would've hated it all," I said.

"Yes, wouldn't he? But it's so wonderful you're doing it. I love you, Ed, just as Johnny did."

Friends

Skitch Henderson once said that I treated everyone with love, an observation that made me sound more like a captain in the Salvation Army instead of a colonel in the U.S. Marines. Well, I haven't always treated *everyone* with love. In 1952, I dropped several unloving things on some North Koreans. But I always felt a little extra love for Johnny, who dropped a few bombs of his own when we were together.

Most comic teams are not good friends or even friends at all. Laurel and Hardy didn't hang out together, Abbott and Costello weren't best of friends, and Dean Martin and Jerry Lewis—well, there were warmer feelings between Custer and Sitting Bull. However, Johnny and I were the happy exception. Although he was my boss, we shared the unwavering affection of a couple of equals who drove themselves to work, finally found the right wives, and liked to lose themselves in drumming and singing while listening to jazz.

For forty-six years, Johnny and I were as close as two non-married people can be. And if he heard me say that, he might say, "Ed, I always felt you were my insignificant other."

On his farewell show, I was deeply moved when Johnny told America, "This show would have been impossible to do without Ed.

From the Author's Collection

An early publicity photo showed that we enjoyed working together.

Some of the best things we've done on the show have just been . . . well, he starts something, I start something . . . Ed has been a rock for thirty years and we've been friends for thirty-four. A lot of people who work together on television don't like each other, but Ed and I have been good friends. You can't fake that on TV."

No, you can't. George Burns said, "In show business, the most important thing is sincerity. And if you can fake that, you've got it made." However, there was no faking what Johnny and I felt for each other.

Every year on our anniversary show, October 1, Johnny would turn to me and say, "I wouldn't be sitting in this chair for [fill in a number from two to thirty] years if it weren't for this man beside me. He's my rock."

My booming laugh on *The Tonight Show* was never just a conditioned reflex, but always a genuine appreciation for the man who could come up with something like: "A woman was arrested out here in Los Angeles for trading sex not for money but for spaghetti dinners. Would that make her a pastatute?"

That line came from Johnny, not one of his writers, none of whom had wit that approached his.

On another night, Madeline Kahn and Johnny were talking about their fears. "Anything particular that you're afraid of?" he asked her.

"Well, it's strange, Johnny," she said, "but I don't like balls coming toward me." "That's called testaphobia," Johnny said.

Johnny always managed to come up with just the right line, or just the right gesture, or a blend of both.

Ice Water?

"Johnny Carson has ice water in his veins," some people used to say.

To which Johnny once replied, "That's just not true; I had all the ice water removed. I did it in Denmark many years ago."

He also had a less comic reply: "Ed, I'm so tired of the same old crap: people telling me, 'You're cool and aloof.' They always want to know why I'm cool and aloof instead of hot and stooped. You've known me for eighteen years. *Am* I cool and aloof?"

"No, my lord."

Johnny had developed the reputation for being cold and aloof because he was uncomfortable with people he didn't know, but I knew him better than anyone outside of his family, and I can tell you there was never any ice water to remove. In July of 1995, when my son Michael died at forty-four from stomach cancer, Johnny called me with just the right words. And after speaking those words, he said, "There's not a day when you won't think of him."

Ice water? When his own son Rick was killed in a car crash in 1991, Johnny gave a short, moving eulogy that let America know what flowed in his veins.

"I'm not doing this to be mawkish, believe me," he said as he showed a picture of Rick and then some of Rick's nature photographs. "Rick was an exuberant young man, fun to be around. And he tried so hard to please. You'll have to forgive a father's pride in these pictures."

The final one was a sunset.

And America knew that warm flow again on the next to last *Tonight Show,* when Bette Midler sang to Johnny and his eyes moistened on

Associated Press, Douglas C. Pizac

May 22, 1992, was the last of nearly five thousand times that Johnny and I sat on opposite sides of the desk on *The Tonight Show.*

hearing "You Made Me Love You" and "One for My Baby and One More for the Road."

That was one of the very few times I saw Johnny tearful. I can remember only three others: at Jack Benny's funeral; when Alex Haley, the author of *Roots,* gave Johnny a leather-bound volume titled *Roots of Johnny Carson—A Tribute to a Great American Entertainer* with the inscription, "With warm wishes to you and your family from the family of Kunta Kinte" on the flyleaf; and when Jimmy Stewart read "I'll Never Forget a Dog Named Beau," a poem about his golden retriever. The poem was forgettable, but Johnny was moved by the way Jimmy Stewart delivered it. Jimmy was a blend of great actor and great person. Both Johnny and I were in tears. Just a couple of maudlin mutt mourners.

Achingly Missed

I don't think I will ever be able to accept that Johnny is gone. His favorite song, "I'll Be Seeing You," is hard for me to hear now, much harder than hearing Stevie Wonder sing it to Johnny on one of the last shows. So often I look at a phone with a sinking feeling because I can't pick it up and get to him.

"And well you know that sinking feeling," Johnny would say, *"from all the nights we went into the tank."*

Johnny Carson is achingly missed. The critic James Wolcott described him as "cool, unflappable, precise, Carson always knew how to pivot. He was comedy's blue diamond, the master practitioner, the model of excellence."

Yes, blue diamond, this large rhinestone remembers well how

you pivoted with all those guests who suddenly made you dance with them. You weren't Fred Astaire, but you weren't Fred Mertz either. You danced endearingly one night with Pearl Bailey to "Love Is Here to Stay," moving with an airy blend of comedy and grace. You danced courageously with Vlasta, the international queen of polka, who easily could have made you look like someone falling down stairs. And the night I watched you rhumba with that fat woman from Detroit, looking funny but not foolish, never mocking her but sweeping her along with that same airy blend, I wondered, *Is there* nothing *this man can't do*?

For more than three decades, we performed together on two television shows and at road shows, conventions, and state fairs. We read each other so well that either of us could launch a bit and the other would know where to take it. When a dog in one of my Alpo commercials walked away from the food instead of eating it, Johnny knew how to jump right in. On all fours, he crawled over to the food bowl and became TV's first animal understudy.

When Johnny said that one of Joan Embrey's chimps was seven or eight years old and I said, "No, Johnny, I think he's nine," we looked at each other and were off on another flight from an unlikely launching pad.

"Let me get this straight, Ed," said Johnny, tapping the pencil he often held. "You're correcting me about the age of a chimp?"

"Sorry, Johnny," I said, playing it just as straight, "but a man has got to have standards. You start with faking the age of chimps and then you fake elephants and the next thing you know, you're five years younger yourself. You just work your way up."

"Or down."

"Yes, that's certainly another way to look at it."

"Ed, you studied philosophy in college and maybe even learned a little. In the grand scheme of things, how important is the age of a chimp?"

"Well, maybe not important to Plato," I said.

"Right. Plato had hamsters."

"But you'll have to admit it's certainly important to the chimp."

"Eight, nine . . . he's too young to drive anyway."

"But not for certain theme park rides, if the cutoff is nine and not eight."

"I have a theme park ride in mind for you, Ed. The half-built roller coaster."

What Was Johnny Really Like?

Since Johnny's death, every national magazine except *Cattleman's Quarterly* has been telling things about him that small children already knew. Well, I'm going to tell you some things that neither small children nor large adults know. Here, with Johnny's nervous blessing, is my answer to the question that almost drove this second banana bananas: What was Johnny really like? And as I spin these memories, I'll be hearing him say, *"Easy on the bull, Ed, or I'll find a way to have Carnac let everyone know that the Marine Corps issued you a security blanket."*

On his last show, Johnny read this line from a letter: "Now we'll see if Ed McMahon *really* thinks you're funny."

A cute line. But for anyone seriously wondering if I were the world's greatest actor for thirty-four years, these pages contain the resounding answer.

two

Good-bye, Mr. Philadelphia Television

Johnny came to New York from a CBS show in Los Angeles called *The Johnny Carson Show*, which was canceled after thirty-nine weeks. Its producer, a man named Brady, said, "Johnny Carson isn't a strong voice. He just can't do stand-up comedy." It couldn't have been an easy thing to do, but Mr. Brady managed to overlook what was already an impressive comic talent. He must have been related to the Hollywood producer who saw Fred Astaire's screen test and said, "Can't sing, can't act—dances a little."

A former carnival barker, boardwalk pitchman, and Marine

Corps pilot in World War II and Korea, I had come from broadcasting at Philadelphia's WCAU, a show so deep in TV's prehistoric age that its eleven o'clock news ended at nine fifteen. The station then became a night-light until the next morning for a city that W. C. Fields saluted on his tombstone with the words: *I'd rather be in Philadelphia.*

It was 1958, and unlike Mr. Brady, the programmers at ABC saw enough in Johnny Carson to make him the host of a daytime game show called *Who Do You Trust?* And one of them saw enough in me to suggest me as an announcer to Johnny. My road to Johnny was long and full of detours and potholes. It led from the boardwalk in Atlantic City, where I sold Morris Metric Slicers; through carnivals, where I boomed enticements for strange acts; and it even took me door-to-door selling pots and pans.

Heeeeere's stainless steel!

Early Rehearsals

I began to prepare for my life with Johnny when I was eight years old. I did more than just lie on a rug and dream of microphones. I turned my grandmother's parlor into a studio where I did my own shows. Those were the golden days of American radio, when the announcers had rich, full voices fit for pulpits. In my boyish voice, I announced everything from the sinking of the *Titanic* to the rising of the sun. And I knew how to introduce, tease, or sum up every fifteen-minute adventure serial on the air.

People who came into the house were startled by the boyish cries:

> From out of the night comes *Bulldog Drummond!* . . . Have you *tried* Wheaties? . . . Heigh-ho, *Silver*, away! . . . This is a job for . . . Superman! . . . Who knows what evil lurks in the hearts of men? The Shadow knows! . . . Jack Armstrong, the all-American boy! . . . L-A-V-A, L-A-V-A . . . I have a lady in the balcony, Doctor . . . Good evening, Mr. and Mrs. North and South America and all the ships at sea. Let's go to press! Flash! Ed McMahon got hit by another nun today!

To my parents, my dream of being a radio announcer was merely a whim, but not to the boy who even announced, "Good morning, Bayonne. It'll be sunny and mild in Hudson County today. There's a twenty-minute delay at the Lincoln Tunnel,

From the Author's Collection

As host of the Miss Philadelphia Contest for the Miss Universe Pageant, I always looked for intellectual depth. Once I almost found it.

fifteen-minute at the Holland, and a great view from the George Washington Bridge. Adolf Hitler just took over Germany."

At seventeen, I had my first job in radio, but I also prepared for Johnny by working as a bingo announcer at carnivals. "Here's the winner—Fannie Schmertz! Come up here, Fannie, and get your forty dollars! Where are you from, dear? Jersey City? What a glamorous place that is!"

My unwavering dream was to be America's greatest radio announcer. I never dreamed, of course, that "I have a lady in the balcony" was rehearsal for feeding El Moldo. And that "Heigh-ho, Silver!" was a prelude to "Hi-yooo!"

"Philadelphia's Mr. Television"

Philadelphians saw more than enough of me in the fifties. In 1952, I had thirteen shows. I was host of the late-night movie, starred on a game show, and did spots on the news. I also had a

McMahon and Company was one of my thirteen Philadelphia television shows. In Philly I did everything but air traffic control.

From the Author's Collection

From the Author's Collection

When I met Marilyn Monroe on the set of *How to Marry a Millionaire*, she told me, "You know, Ed, I don't have anything on under this." But, of course, I saw right through that.

show called *Strictly for the Girls* and played a clown on a Saturday morning circus show called *The Big Top.*

Yes, I did everything on local television but describe the traffic on the Pennsylvania Turnpike. The magazine that would become *TV Guide* called me "Philadelphia's Mr. Television." Of course, W. C. Fields would have said, "Being Philadelphia's Mr. Television is almost as great an honor as being Newark's Mr. Mail."

And then the Marine Corps recalled me and sent me to Korea. My recall was a double jeopardy faced by many reserve officers who were transferred from warm beds to cold mountains after North Korea decided that five years of peace were too many. Ensign Johnny Carson, who dreamed of becoming a professional magician, was lucky—there was less need in combat for men who knew how to make the three of spades disappear.

During World War II, I served my first tour of duty in the Marines, learning how to fly and then teaching flying and carrier landing to others, including some of Pappy Boyington's pilots, who went on to lead the famous Black Sheep squadron. Now the Marines were asking me back to see an exotic Asian land and for a chance to get killed there. I put on my uniform again, bought some life insurance, and flew into the unfriendly North Korean skies. New "critics" were gunning for me now—and they hadn't seen any of my shows. It was my great fortune that all of them missed during the eighty-five combat missions I flew.

I returned from Korea to a heartwarming welcome. All thirteen of my shows had been canceled. And so, every morning, I took the eight o'clock train to New York, where I went into my office—a Penn Station phone booth—took out a five dollar roll of dimes and index cards, and called agents, talent scouts, and producers to try to get a TV audition. On most days, after not getting one, I took an early train back to Philadelphia for my only TV work—a five-minute commentary at the end of the local nightly news. Regular commuters knew how my day had gone. If I took the 4:30 Congressional back, an audition had opened for me. Most days, however, I took an earlier train back to Philadelphia to keep dreaming the seemingly impossible dream.

three

"Thanks for Coming Up, Ed!"

My audition with Johnny for *Who Do You Trust?* was the happy result of where I happened to live. The old real estate cry of "location, location, location!" describes what delivered me to Johnny and all that followed. In 1958, I was living in the town of Drexel Hill, just outside of Philadelphia, where Dick Clark was my neighbor.

One day, Edward R. Murrow's *Person to Person* show came to Drexel Hill to do a program with Dick, for whom my daughter Claudia had done some babysitting. It was the biggest thing to hit Drexel Hill since the British were thrown out.

When Murrow's taping ended, my friend Dan Kelly—who found me the apartment next to Dick Clark—said, "Ed, come on

Globe Photos, Inc.

Edward R. Murrow's *Person to Person* was indirectly responsible for my meeting Johnny. When Murrow came to Pennsylvania to do a show with Dick Clark, I met Chuck Reeves, who recommended me for *Who Do You Trust?*

down tonight to a party we're having at the club." It was a private club at the garden apartment complex.

And so I attended the party, and I was having a wonderful time until Dan suddenly said to me, "Ed, get up and entertain!"

"Get up and *what?*" I asked.

"Get up on *stage.*"

I probably had absorbed enough alcohol to lose track of the fact that I had no act. What could I do to entertain? Imitations of jets taking off? Introductions of tattooed ladies? My Atlantic City pitch for the Morris Metric Slicer? I found, however, the dumb nerve to walk onto that stage, where I settled for telling some jokes that the crowd graciously pretended were funny.

When my act mercifully ended, Chuck Reeves, Dick Clark's producer, came over to me. Chuck's New York office was in the Little Theater, next door to the theater where Johnny Carson was about to do *Who Do You Trust?* I had learned enough at Catholic University to know that the show should have been called *Whom Do*

You Trust? but ABC's biggest daytime demographic wasn't people in love with grammar.

I thought my act had been "just okay," but Chuck thought otherwise.

"You were great!" he said, revealing that he must have had more to drink than I had. "Have you ever thought about going to New York?"

"Just every second of every minute of every hour of every day," I replied.

"I'll remember that," he said. "I'll call you."

Those words are usually as meaningful as "the check is in the mail."

A Promise Kept

Chuck did remember, however, and one day outside of his New York office he overheard Art Stark, the producer of *Who Do You Trust?*, saying, "Well, we've got to replace him. We've got to find another announcer."

"Wait a minute!" Chuck called to Art Stark. "I've got the guy for you! He's in Philadelphia and he's perfect."

"Who is he?"

"Ed McMahon."

"Never heard of him."

"I'll have him here tomorrow morning."

By this time—September of 1958—I had moved to a lovely new house that I had built in Gulph Mills. Guided by destiny, I gave my daughter Claudia her own phone as a present for her thirteenth birthday. My phone was unlisted, but Claudia's wasn't; and so,

Chuck Reeves was able to find me through her and said, "Ed, you have to get right up to New York! I have a great job for you with Johnny Carson!"

Imagine if I had given Claudia a puppy!

Johnny Carson was someone I had seen many times. I did a show at night in Philadelphia, and on Wednesday nights Johnny was on with a New York variety show that I watched all that summer. And I liked what I saw: a supremely poised young man who was consistently fresh and funny. I liked not just his wit but his body movements too. He was instinctively entertaining in everything he said and did.

A few days later, on a street just east of Times Square, I walked into Johnny's dressing room and said, "I'm Ed McMahon"—words I had said thousands of times on the air as if rehearsing for this moment.

"Glad you could come up, Ed," said Johnny, warmly shaking my hand.

Did he think I was doing *him* a favor by wanting to stop being the darling of the Delaware Valley so I could talk to the rest of America on ABC?

I knew my odds for being chosen as announcer were just slightly better than the odds on the bull pulling an upset against the toreador. In spite of his warmth, Johnny sounded to me like a casting director giving a reflex welcome to an actor whose audition was a pointless one.

Two of the windows in Johnny's dressing room overlooked Forty-fourth Street and had a view of a theater down the street, whose entire marquee was being changed for a new show called *The Bells Are Ringing* that starred Judy Holliday. As Johnny and I

From the Author's Collection

I even got experience as a quiz show host in New York, which would serve me well for the years I was announcer on *Who Do You Trust?*

watched four giant cranes lift the big billboard that was to be the new marquee, he asked, "Where'd you go to school, Ed?"

"Catholic University," I said.

"Has a fine drama school, doesn't it?"

"Yes, excellent."

Was he going to ask me to recite some of *Macbeth*?

"What are you doing now?"

"I've got a couple of shows in Philadelphia—variety shows that I host."

He paused for a moment, looked out the window, and said, "Just look at that marquee, Ed. Broadway will never be the same. It's changed forever."

"It certainly has," I said, flaunting my intelligence.

"You came up on the train from Philadelphia?"

"Yes, I did."

And then, he shook my hand again and said, "Well, thanks very much for coming up, Ed. It was good meeting you."

My six minutes with Johnny were over; and translating his last words, I heard: *Don't call us, we'll call you. But not in this lifetime.*

I went back to Philadelphia, certain I had blown the audition, wondering what else I could have done to impress Johnny and Art Stark—told them how I had saved them from the North Koreans?

four

The Warmest Welcome

It was only years later, deep into *The Tonight Show,* that I learned Johnny had made up his mind the moment he saw me to move me above seven other candidates and make me his announcer for *Who Do You Trust?* By then, I knew that this was his style—he always knew instantly what he liked and he went for it at once.

Of course, on the Friday after my six-minute interview, I had no idea that my Philadelphia days were over. In fact, on Monday I was scheduled to go to Europe with the winner of a contest held by the sponsor of one of my shows. My wife didn't want to go, but I decided to take my daughter Claudia and show her some of the glories of the old world. My ESP must have been working overtime because suddenly something made me cancel that trip.

Just two hours later, that "something" was on the phone, saying,

"Hi, Ed, this is Art Stark. When you show up, we want you to wear a suit."

"A suit?" I asked, the way I would later repeat Aunt Blabby's last words.

"Yes, Johnny wants to wear sports clothes, and we want to emphasize your size when you're next to him."

"But . . . what are you talking about?" I asked.

"Oh, didn't they call you? You got the job; you start next Monday."

I had been dreaming of a job like this since I was a small boy in Philadelphia pretending that a flashlight was a microphone. Now, however, in addition to liking my voice, Art Stark liked the contrast between a six-foot-four, 220-pound Irishman and the Midwestern WASP of whom there was considerably less. It had seemed like forever since my visit to Johnny—waiting for a phone call that I was certain would never come.

Who Do You Trust?

On Monday, October 13, 1958, I began work as Johnny's announcer on *Who Do You Trust?* The game was the least important aspect of the show. It was simply a vehicle that allowed Johnny Carson to show off his genius. My job was to introduce the contestants, do the commercials, and have occasional brief conversations with Johnny at the top of the show. When I came out for the first time, Johnny established a relationship that would last for almost fifty years. Pretending not to see me, he suddenly turned and said in surprise, "Lothar, you startled me!"

Nate Cutler/Globe Photos

Johnny and I had many wonderful memories, both on and off the show. On his farewell show, Johnny said, "A lot of people who work together on television don't like each other, but Ed and I have been good friends. You can't fake that on TV."

You may be thinking that Lothar is the president of Sri Lanka, but he was the huge manservant to a cartoon character named Mandrake the Magician. Johnny was announcing that the big guy and the little guy—well, reverse that billing—were on their way.

He then gave me a memorably warm welcome: he set fire to my script. As I was about to make my announcement for the first of six sponsors whose copy lines were on a sheet of paper in my hand, Johnny decided they all could go to blazes. And from that day on, whenever I began to read the opening announcement, he set fire to the bottom of my script, and so I had to read the opening as fast as I could before all the words burned up. No announcer ever had such a trial by fire. I was the first one who ever read charcoal. Of course, Johnny's little cookout got a huge laugh.

I do not exaggerate about this particular little conflagration. And because Johnny thought that torching my copy had gone so well, he actually did it on every taping of the show for the next four years! I had to memorize all the copy and wing it as well as I could, hoping that at least I got the names right. If the copy said, "Keebler chocolate chip cookies with the big extra chips are absolutely delicious," the fire edited my text to "Keebler . . . absolutely." If the copy said, "Dristan is the miracle for your eustachian tube," I managed, "Dristan . . . for your tube."

Johnny wanted to enjoy the sight of *me* treading water in the tube, instinctively knowing I was professional enough not to go under. One of those sponsors should have been Zippo.

In those four years of *Who Do You Trust?* Johnny and I shaped our unique relationship on the air. I set up the jokes and he got the laughs, sometimes at my expense. One day, he crawled under the camera and gave me a hot foot while I was doing a spot, distracting me so much that instead of saying, "StayPuff makes it easy to pin a diaper," I said, "StayPuff makes it easy to pee."

"I think there's something wrong with him," my wife said one day.

"No," I said, "there's something very right."

"Why does he think you're a barbecue?"

"He knows exactly what I am."

"Well, I hate for the children to see you on fire."

"I wonder if there's a suit my size in asbestos."

I also wondered if Mr. Brady saw how quickly Johnny was smoking in every way on *Who Do You Trust?* On one of the early shows, a contestant was telling Johnny at great length about a pregnant armadillo she had and how happy it was to "be with armadillo." Johnny was clearly bored by this report of scaly gestation, and I could see that the woman was an anesthetic for the audience too. The appeal of maternity doesn't really pick up until you've moved higher than camels.

Suddenly, Johnny asked the woman, "Tell me, how come you know these things if you're not an armadillo?"

Another time, one of the contestants was a Latin Quarter showgirl wearing a poured-on dress, Day-Glo makeup, and a hairdo that could have crowned Miss American Hooker.

"On your way to a Four-H Club meeting, are you?" asked Johnny, and I knew that I was on my way too.

He's got it, I thought. *This man thinks funny. I've hitched my wagon to a star.*

One day the jackpot question for a young couple was "Give the difference between an African elephant and an Indian one."

I don't remember if the couple gave the right answer, but I do remember what Johnny said: "Well, at least they don't visit each other. Not too many African elephants in New Delhi. Or *any* deli. They don't need more tongue."

This, I thought, *is going to be fun. I'm tied to a wit as fast as Groucho's.*

For another couple, the jackpot question was "Name the female flier who was lost in the South Pacific."

After that couple had correctly answered, "Amelia Earhart," Johnny said, "You know . . . Amelia Earhart was more like a guy. Most women would have stopped at Guam for directions."

And then there was the jackpot question that was a remarkable preview of things to come. The question was "Name the man who explored North America before Columbus."

The answer was Eric the Red. After a woman gave the answer, Johnny offered the smile that would enchant America and said, "That could also be the answer to 'What did the Nixon committee call Eric?'"

Neither of us knew it, but Carnac the Magnificent was being born.

Another day, after Johnny had given the audience a few such gems, I said to him, "Johnny, you're a natural. I don't understand how your CBS show could have failed."

"Because they wouldn't *let* me be natural," he replied. "Our reviews were good, but the network people wanted higher ratings and I was dumb enough to let them start telling me what to do. 'We've got to make the show *important*,' they said. Now how the hell were they going to do *that*? Have me come on to 'God Save the Queen'? They wanted a funny Edward R. Murrow. Ed, I'm an entertainer—no more, no less. I learned the hard way that you have to follow your own instincts."

"And also," I said, "anyone who never fails can never have success."

"You've been eating Chinese."

"Well, I know you're a funny guy. And your interviewing is great. You've got the curiosity of a child."

"You mean a child who's curious. I know some curious children. And I know some who are just plain strange."

Fearless

Yes, from the beginning, Johnny knew precisely what he was and he stayed true to it. He was as unpretentiously brilliant as Noël Coward, who described his own gift as "a talent to amuse." And

Courtesy of Stephen Cox Collection

Johnny enjoyed sparring with the Chairman of the Board, whether on *The Tonight Show* or in Jilly's.

Johnny had the self-confidence of Coward. In fact, he was fearless—of man or beast.

Jim Fowler, an animal trainer, once brought a tarantula to the show and put him on Johnny's hand. With a sick smile, Johnny asked, "He's poisonous, right?"

"Not *that* poisonous," Fowler said.

"So I won't be *that* dead," said Johnny.

"Just don't anger him."

"How am I going to make a tarantula angry? By saying, 'You're ugly'?"

"By blowing on him."

"I never blow on a tarantula," Johnny said. "That's one of the things my mother taught me."

And Johnny was unafraid of something even scarier than the tarantula—Frank Sinatra.

Johnny's courage was burned into my memory one night early in the run of *The Tonight Show.* It was well past midnight and we were sitting in the piano bar of a Manhattan restaurant called Jilly's, basking in the glow of vodka sours and looking forward to our two-man jam session of voice and drums. Suddenly, Frank Sinatra came in and the congregation fell silent, for Sinatra's appearance in Jilly's was a religious experience. Everyone just watched in reverence as His Holiness walked past the bar. No one would dare speak to him unless he spoke first. No one wanted to be turned into salt. And then, throughout the restaurant the voice of Johnny Carson was heard: "Dammit, Frank," he said, "I told you ten thirty!"

five

A Party of One

While I was still living in Gulph Mills, Pennsylvania, I decided to throw a surprise party for Johnny, a risky event to spring on a man who liked to party only with the entire country. Because Gulph Mills was near Radnor, the home of *TV Guide,* I told Johnny that *TV Guide* wanted him to pose for a cover picture in front of their headquarters.

"Ed, you know how I feel about posing for stills," he said. "It's so damn tedious; you just sit around for hours. Let 'em give the cover to Jackie Gleason."

"Yes, I know your attention span," I said. "I promise I'll make them take it fast. We'll pick up some Valium on the way."

"Can't they take the picture on the set?"

"They'd rather have you come to their office," I said, hoping that he wouldn't ask me to explain such an illogical point.

"And get all the ambiance of Radnor?" Johnny asked.

"It'll be easy this way. Just pick me up and we'll go together."

"They want *your* picture *too*? It's getting less appealing by the minute." His look turned dubious. "Ed, I don't know . . ."

But I knew: I had arranged for Johnny's brother, sister, brother-in-law, kids—and about thirty others he loved—to be at my house to surprise him. It would be a better party if he came.

At one o'clock the following day, Johnny walked through my front door.

"Let's go out to the pool," I said. "I want to show you something."

"Got a new supply of algae, do you?" he asked.

How I now wanted to say, "Heeeeere's Johnny!" How greatly I feared that he would take one look at the crowd of fifty people and keep walking to Bryn Mawr. He came out, however, everyone cried "Surprise!" and for a few seconds he smiled silently. And then his eyes began to tear. Ice water? It was warm and salty.

You can't script a party and you can't set up any TV improvisation. A party is a first draft; Johnny's monologue was a tenth. The man who endlessly studied tapes of his old shows couldn't prepare that way for a party, where he felt uneasy with just a few people instead of the millions who gave him his high. Johnny's social life *was* his monologue.

When Johnny was interviewing a guest, he remembered every word the guest had said. However, there was one thing that I found he had often forgotten; whether he had eaten. Perhaps he had that nice slim build because he had no deep interest in food. In fact, he barely had a shallow one.

"Ed, I can't remember if I had lunch," he told me one day, saying this to a man who at breakfast was envisioning dinner. At dinner in Danny's Hideaway, he liked to tell the waiter, "I want a steak, but not one of those thick ones. Just a very thin one."

He wanted a breakfast steak at dinner. Johnny had been a naval officer, but he was a man who might not have minded sitting down to a plate of Spam.

Sometimes he ordered only a salad and some mineral water. And sometimes he drank something called Weight On, which I tasted once and it struck me as the ideal drink to make a suspect confess.

I, however, often ordered thick pork chops smothered in cinnamon applesauce. Johnny was so oblivious to the meals we ate together that one night in Danny's, he asked, "You know what you can order here, Ed?"

"What, Johnny?" I said.

Courtesy of Stephen Cox Collection

Here I am with Dick Clark, my Philadelphia neighbor, who helped me get out of the neighborhood.

"Thick pork chops with applesauce."

This from one of the fastest wits in the history of show business!

The speed of his wit was never shown better than the time I heard a fan ask him, "What made you a star?"

Johnny's answer could have been chiseled in stone at the Comedy Club: "I started out in a gaseous state and then I cooled."

Making It Look Easy

Everyone thought Johnny was so cool, and he was—on the surface. But Johnny the Perfectionist was tense underneath. Only I saw the cigarette burning under his desk every night and the endless drumming with a couple of pencils that he liked to hold.

"People think I'm always so relaxed," he once told me, "but the truth is I'm always nervous. Making it look easy is a hell of a strain."

Johnny had this temperament in common with many great writers and composers, who knew the enormous effort required to produce a seemingly effortless result. I remember that one of the great composers—I think it was Franz Joseph Haydn, but it might have been Barry Manilow—did a hundred drafts of a melody simple enough to be hummed by children.

And I had to make my own role on the show look effortless too. Of course, people weren't always sure what I was making look effortless. I was able to be a ripe second banana for Johnny because I had spent years studying the brilliant wit of *The Tonight Show*'s father, Steve Allen.

"Do they get your show in Philadelphia?" a woman in the audience once asked Steve.

NBC/Globe Photos, Inc.

Steve Allen, father of *The Tonight Show,* was a tough act to follow. Only Johnny could have done it.

"They see it but they don't get it," he replied, setting a standard for ad-libbed wit that only Johnny Carson would reach.

I studied the smooth and knowledgeable way that Steve interviewed guests, his spontaneous wackiness with them, and the goofy characters he created. I knew that Johnny also loved Steve, and so the format of our show became the one this master had invented. Johnny might have forgotten if he'd eaten, but he never forgot Steve and, with his own rich originality, he took off in all the directions that Steve had charted—except one: Johnny never put his wife on the show the way Steve Allen once used Jayne Meadows.

Perhaps Johnny had seen what happened at that particular family presentation. Jayne was singing a song—that is, she was trying to. When Steve walked up to her, she said, "I'm not finished."

"Yes, you are," he said and there was the kind of laugh that Johnny would be getting for thirty years, the kind Johnny got when a man suddenly ran nude across the set.

"He won't be prosecuted," Johnny said. "The case will be dismissed for lack of evidence."

In thousands of lines like that, Jack Benny's prophecy was fulfilled: "That Carson kid is just great," Benny said when Johnny was still at CBS. "You better watch him."

Like Steve Allen, Johnny had unique verbal and physical skills. I don't know who was Steve's idol, but I know that Johnny honed his own skills by studying the timing of his idol Jack Benny.

"I used to lie on the rug with my face in my hands and listen to him," Johnny told me. "That's when I knew what I wanted to do. I wanted to grow up and get laughs just the way Benny did, with those wonderful pauses."

"I was lying on a different rug," I said, "wanting to be Don Wilson."

Don Wilson was Benny's big jolly announcer, whose "Jellooooo again!" might have been a subconscious inspiration for my "Heeeeere's Johnny!"

six

Not Below Paar

By mid-1962, after *Who Do You Trust?* had been on the air for four years, NBC began looking for a replacement for the star of *The Tonight Show,* Jack Paar.

The Tonight Show had been born on May 29, 1950, under the name of *Broadway Open House.* The alternating hosts of this live show were two nightclub comics, Jerry Lester and Morey Amsterdam, but the most memorable performer was a blonde more than six feet tall named Dagmar, who, to use the correct words, pointed the way to Carol Wayne on Johnny's *Tea Time Movie.* Had Dagmar been with the much shorter Johnny on *Tea Time Movie,* he would have stood in the shade and thought of the La Leche League.

In more ways than one, Dagmar was on a higher level than the rest of *Broadway Open House,* which I often saw after doing my own thirteen shows in Philadelphia.

The gang of *Broadway Open House*, the forerunner of *The Tonight Show*. Left to right are announcer Wayne Howell, emcee Jerry Lester, and bandleader Milton DeLugg. At the right is Dagmar, who got more than her share from puberty.

Courtesy of Stephen Cox Collection

"I just came through muck and mire," someone told Jerry Lester one night.

"Hi, Muck," Lester said. "Where's Myer?"

That joke had first been told by Columbus, giving his men a second reason to mutiny.

I wonder if this show will ever be replaced by a professional one, I thought.

In 1953, *Broadway Open House* was transformed into *The Steve Allen Show,* a local NBC show in New York whose bespectacled star opened with a monologue and then went into the studio audience for exchanges like this with his own mother:

Steve: "Tell me, what's your profession?"

Mother: "I'm a Holy Roller."

Steve: "No, that's your belief. I mean your *profession.* For example, *I* am an entertainer."

Mother: "That's your belief."

On September 27, 1954, *The Steve Allen Show* joined the full NBC network as *The Tonight Show*, where Steve said in his opening monologue at 11:15, "You think you're tired now? Wait till 1:00 A.M. rolls around."

"Hi ho, Steverino!" Louis Nye, one of the show's regulars, was exclaiming while I was dreaming of being part of such a midnight merriness. It was during Steve Allen's tenure on *The Tonight Show* that Skitch Henderson—who was with Johnny for his first five years—joined the show. When Steve Allen left, NBC let Ernie Kovacs host the show for a few months and then tried a show called *America After Dark*, which was deeply in the dark about how to entertain.

Jack Paar took over *The Tonight Show* in July 1957, but by 1962, Jack—who had been witty, offbeat, and controversial—always seemed to be on the brink of a nervous breakdown on the air.

"I knew Doris Day before she was a virgin," Jack's guest Oscar Levant said one night.

Johnny says things like that on every show, I thought.

Jack Paar's unburdening himself did have a certain fascination, like an overturned tractor-trailer. One night, he cried on the show because his daughter Randi got her first training bra. Johnny, who had been a guest host for Paar several times, would have handled such an event without tears. Instead, with dry, quizzical eyes, he might have said something like, "My daughter just got a training bra. That is, I *think* it's a training bra. It might be a tourniquet."

Paar could present the human comedy in a funny and touching way, but his comic regulars were mere imitations of what Johnny would be all by himself. One of Paar's regulars was an actress named Dody Goodman, who did a scatterbrained act. It would take Johnny as Aunt Blabby to make a ditsy woman funny.

Another regular was Cliff Arquette, who played a rumpled rube. It would take Johnny as Floyd R. Turbo to give a rube comic elevation with lines like, "The draft is good for the country. It will take crime off the streets and put it in the army where it belongs."

When NBC wanted to replace Jack Paar, whose naked psyche was leaving too many viewers uneasy, the network turned to Johnny, whose wit was delivered by a cool and composed man of thirty-six. Ironically, Johnny was as nervous as Paar, but his nervousness was always concealed—to almost everyone but me. I kept seeing it off camera.

"Ed, it's the smoking," he told me, "and I just can't kick it. I should go to some place where they get you to quit by shocking you or making you watch endless reruns of *Gilligan's Island*. You know what I should tell the kids? If you must smoke, don't do it orally."

Courtesy of Stephen Cox Collection

Skitch Henderson, who led *The Tonight Show* band for Jack Paar and for Johnny until 1966.

Johnny, however, didn't jump at NBC's enticing offer. He had self-confidence, but he wasn't as good a prophet as Carnac.

"I don't think I can cut it, Ed," he told me one day as we tested the vodka at Sardi's to make sure that no healthful impurities had gotten into it.

NBC/Globe Photos

Jack Parr and Hugh Downs, the last time Jack hosted *The Tonight Show* and just before I filled the air with "Heeeeere's Johnny!"

"Of course you can," I said. "It's absolutely perfect for you."

I sounded as though I were doing a commercial: selling Johnny to himself.

"I can handle a half-hour daytime quiz," he said, "but the jump to an hour and forty-five minutes at night . . . well, that jump feels like one from a bridge. People are telling me I'd be nuts to replace Paar."

"I'm not one of them," I said, amazed that Johnny had such reservations.

"I can just hear everyone making the same joke: *Carson is under Paar.*"

"Your jokes are better than that and you know it," I said. "Johnny, you're ready. And you owe yourself the chance to reach a big night audience."

At last, his manager, Al Bruno, convinced him to take the job, where Johnny was to work for ninety minutes in an old radio studio on the sixth floor of the NBC Building at Rockefeller Center. Although his manager and I had talked Johnny into taking the job, I had forgotten to talk him into taking *me* with him. Would anyone else be doing that? There was a play running called *Philadelphia, Here I Come!* I wondered if it was about me.

As Johnny headed for *Tonight Show* glory, I presumed that the rumors were true: his announcer would be Jack Paar's Hugh Downs. Hugh was a splendid announcer and a highly intelligent man, whose mind I had admired during his work with Paar. One of my thirteen Philadelphia shows, *McMahon and Company*, had followed Paar—for people who wanted to be eased to sleep.

One night while I was presuming that *The Tonight Show* would be passing up my intangible appeal and instead going for Hugh Downs, I was standing at the bar in Sardi's with Johnny. We were celebrating that it was Thursday. We also liked to celebrate the Constitution, Arbor Day, and the invention of indoor plumbing.

"You know, Ed," said Johnny, "I've been thinking . . ."

"I've tried that from time to time," I said. "But too much of it can be trouble."

"I've been thinking that when we take over the show . . ."

"You mean *The Tonight Show*?"

"No, *The Shari Lewis Show*. Of course *The Tonight Show*."

"And you said when *we* take over?"

"Of course. You're going with me. Didn't you know that?"

"Certainly. I must have just forgotten."

"Yes, I guess it's hard to remember every little thing."

"Well, Johnny, I'll drink to that!"

"And to daylight savings time," he said.

seven

"Heeeeere's Johnny!" and "Hi-Yooo!"

While he hosted *Who Do You Trust?* the name Johnny Carson was hardly a household word. One evening in the spring of 1960, Johnny and I were having dinner at Sardi's, a restaurant in Manhattan's theater district with walls covered by caricatures of show business stars. When we were almost finished with our meal, our waitress approached the table.

"Would you like more coffee?" she asked me.

"Yes, please," I said.

She refilled my cup and then walked away, ignoring Johnny.

"I see you're dining alone," he said, and then he looked up at the walls and said, "My picture won't be there. I'll have to go for a post office."

Another time at Sardi's we noticed two ladies at a nearby table who were looking at us and smiling.

"You go," we heard one of them say.

"No, you go," said the other.

"No, Helen, you."

As Helen rose and approached us, Johnny and I braced ourselves for an autograph request. When Helen reached us, she asked, "If you're not using the cream, may we have it?"

Athough we didn't know it, *The Tonight Show* would be ending any wish for privacy that Johnny or I might have had.

In Search of Laughter

Just before taping time at NBC on Monday, October 1, 1962, three weeks short of his thirty-seventh birthday, Johnny left his seventh-floor office, picked me up, and we started walking down the stairs together into the unknown.

Supplied by NBC/Globe Photos, Inc.

Dolly Parton, who also had a big heart, let Johnny know that every part of her was real.

"Johnny," I said to him, "this may not be the best time to be asking this particular question, but I really don't know what my role on the show will be."

"I don't know my role either," he replied. "Let's just go down and entertain the hell out of them."

That was the only advice I ever got from him, but that was enough. "Let's just entertain the hell out of them" became the guiding spirit, the fundamental philosophy, of *The Tonight Show.* Both Johnny and I instinctively knew that we were two explorers in search of laughter and there were no maps.

We went on the air, he was introduced by Groucho Marx, there was great applause, and then Johnny came out and said his first words: "Boy, you would think it was Vice President Nixon."

He then went on to say, "Seriously, ladies and gentlemen, this is kind of an emotional thing for me. I don't mean to be maudlin, but I know that a lot of people are watching all over the country. I have only one feeling as I stand here before so many people. *I want my na-na.*"

A Lovable Bad Boy

Johnny was able to entertain the hell out of them for thirty years because he was the best thing an entertainer can be: an original. And he was not just an original but such a natural one that the work behind the wit never showed, just as no fan ever saw the effort beneath Joe DiMaggio's gracefulness. Johnny was probably the only man in show business who could have these easy exchanges with Dolly Parton, and Raquel Welch:

"You know, Johnny," said Dolly, "people are always asking me if they're real."

She wasn't referring to her teeth.

"Oh, I would never do that," Johnny said with his bad boy grin.

"Well, I'll tell you."

"Must you?"

"These are mine."

"Both of them?"

"Both."

"Dolly, I do have guidelines on this show, but I'd give a year's pay to peek under there."

With Raquel Welch, mere innuendo was enough for the laugh. Seated close to him, Raquel was wearing a blouse that left no doubt about her gender. After Johnny had made some quick retort to her, she said, "Oh, that's good."

"Yes," he said, "any opening at all, I jump right in." And then the puckish grin and "Oh-oh."

Johnny loved sexual jokes and always knew precisely how bold they could be because he had a special "lewdness license" as the lovable bad boy from the prairie—the boy who said, "When turkeys make love, they think of swans."

Tea Time Movie

One of the running characters that Johnny played was Art Fern, the idiotic host of *Tea Time Movie.* However, Art Fern was smart enough to have beside him a sometime—well, really almost no time—actress named Carol Wayne, a young woman who had received more than her share from puberty. In a moving salute to her bosoms, Johnny said, "She could have nursed Wyoming."

Courtesy of Stephen Cox Collection

Johnny as Art Fern with Carol Wayne who brought an extra dimension to *Tea Time Movie*.

In one *Tea Time Movie* spot, Carol came out with the model of a house in front of her chest and Art asked the audience, "How would you like to get your hands on one of these?"

Moments later, she was holding a fan of insurance policies, as Art delicately said, "Take a look at what we cover with these policies. And then take a look at what we don't."

In another *Tea Time Movie* spot, Johnny said that Carol would never drown because she carried her own life buoys. In tragic irony, drowning is precisely how Carol died in a Mexican bay early in 1984. Her replacement, Teresa Ganzel, was pretty and played well with Johnny, but she lacked a certain dimension.

Because he had the face of a fallen choirboy, when Johnny used suggestive material, he was able to get big laughs with obvious lines. One night, a female pretzel maker was showing him how to shape the strands. Johnny tried it, but couldn't twist his strand into a pretzel.

"I don't think yours is long enough," she said.

"I've heard that before," said Johnny.

And the audience roared, even though most of them had heard this obvious wordplay many times before.

Because of the special license given to his distinctive style, Johnny always knew exactly how far into blueness he could go—territory he again visited when a butterfly collector came to the show and showed Johnny a few specimens under glass.

"I mounted all these," he proudly said.

"How do you mount a butterfly?" asked Johnny. "It must be very difficult."

The gag was moderately amusing, but another obvious one and one other comics might have come to. But Johnny's look, an endearingly funny blend of angel and devil, was what lifted the line to detonate laughter.

As Planned as a Food Fight

"Ed," he once told me early in our New York run, "I know we've got all these writers, but let's never do anything that sounds like it's had a lot of planning."

"Don't worry, Johnny," I said. "This show feels as planned as a food fight."

"Let's keep it that way," Johnny said. "I don't want to come out with something that smacks of a month's preparation; I couldn't keep that up every night. I'm just going to be my natural self and we'll see what happens."

What happened was the high-water mark of American TV, especially when Johnny threw Don Rickles into a hot tub.

"He's Gonna Entertain Us!"

Johnny acted less like a star than any star I have ever known, although he was always aware of his place on the public scene. He drove himself to the studio alone, carrying his lunch in a paper bag. It was probably the only time anyone had ever brown-bagged it in a white Corvette.

One evening, we dropped into a nightclub to catch the act of a young comedian. We had barely sat down at our table when a large man came over to us. The look on his face told me that he wasn't looking for an autograph. After hovering over us for a few seconds, he pulled Johnny up by one of his arms and dragged him to a table full of his friends—although it was surprising that a man like this *had* any friends. While I wondered which way I would throw him, he turned to the people in the club and cried, "Hey, everyone! This is the great Johnny Carson! He's gonna entertain us!"

I could see that Johnny also wanted to rip into the guy, in spite of the gentleman's size; but Johnny knew the newspaper stories he would be creating, and so he turned to me and said, "Ed, let's get out of here."

Furiously, he twisted away from the guy and we returned to our table, where we decided that the evening had already been more than enough fun and it was time to leave while Johnny was still conscious. Johnny was well aware that all his improvisation had to be with his tongue, not his fists. Or course, after fighting back against any of the large fools who came after him in bars, Johnny might have seen stories about the length of his convalescence.

"HEEEEERE'S JOHNNY!"

As the date of Johnny's first *Tonight Show* approached, I had been thinking hard of a unique way to introduce him. For Jack Paar, Hugh Downs had said, "And yours truly, Hugh Downs." But "yours truly, Hugh Downs" just didn't feel right for me, and it just didn't seem enough to say, "And now, Johnny Carson."

And then, just before Johnny and I walked down one flight to

When I walked onto the first *Tonight Show*, I walked into a thirty-year dream.

From the Author's Collection

NBC's sixth-floor studio that first time, I remembered when I had been doing early radio that I had a clever way of introducing people whose names contained *R*s: I richly rolled the *R*s in those names.

Well, the gods must have been smiling at me because out of my big mouth on that first show came a cry to stand beside "Heigh-ho, Silver!" as one of the most memorable phrases in television history. To several million Americans, I said, "Heeeeere's Johnny!"

The slight pause between my bellow and Johnny's name was less dramatic than Edward R. Murrow's "This . . . is London," but our show was less important than World War II.

"Hi-yooo!"

How did my "Hi-yooo!" come to be, you are asking? Even if you're not, and even if you're asking instead when I'll be bringing you ten million dollars that I keep saying you may already have won from the American Family Publishers, here's the story of the birth of "Hi-yooo!" It may not be as memorable as "Don't give up the ship," but it does have more punch than "Tickets, please."

One night in our seventh year, we had a terrible audience. That night, the studio had all the merriment of Grant's Tomb. You may feel that performers shouldn't blame an audience for a lack of response, but a show *is* a collaboration. Just before the opening night of Oscar Wilde's *The Importance of Being Earnest,* a friend said, "Oscar, I hope the show is a success." And Wilde replied, "The show is already a success. I hope the audience is."

On this particular night, in our seventh year, the audience was failing and I felt they should have been made to stay after school and watch a repeat of the show.

Standing near me just off camera was our associate producer, John Carsey. Suddenly, John raised his fist and said, as a kind of rallying cry, "Hi-yooo!" as if he were not John Carsey but John Wayne putting the wagons in a circle. I had been considering a different cry, like "Wake up, you sluggards!" but John's somehow felt even better and I cried it loudly to the semiconscious crowd. Instantly, they came alive and transformed themselves into a little bit of New Year's Eve in Times Square.

From that night on, I sprinkled every show with a few "Hi-yooos!" Little did I realize when I dreamed of being in radio that I would bring to television a sound that might have been the last one heard by General Custer.

eight

A Chicken Asleep

It was a happy coincidence that one of the guests on Johnny's first *Tonight Show* was Groucho Marx, as if his torch were being passed to Johnny. Also on that first show were Joan Crawford and Rudy Vallee, two people who enriched the meaning of the word *ego.* But for ninety minutes, they were gently upstaged by a Puck from the prairie.

When the show was over, I sensed that we had a hit, but I wasn't sure. For a moment, I wondered if I should go to Johnny's dressing room, where everyone had gone; but then I decided not to and went home, where I soon learned that Johnny was America's newest star.

And a little lightning had struck me too. The following day, one person after another came up to me and said, "Heeeeere's Johnny!"

From the night of that first show to the last show thirty years later, Johnny never gave me a single piece of direction. At each show, in the few minutes before I went out to warm up the audience, he and I talked in his dressing room—about the news of the day and the stock market and our kids and the particular mental illness that made Dodger fans leave the ballpark in the seventh inning, even of a no-hitter. But we never talked about the show.

Those few minutes with Johnny were always an elixir for me. No matter how sick I may have been—and I did the show with every kind of flu from Hong Kong to Jersey City—Johnny was a shot of adrenaline that both relaxed and recharged me.

Johnny's Genius

It didn't take long for Johnny's genius to be revealed to America. Millions quickly learned how brilliant he was with an ad-lib, a saver, or a topper.

When Groucho Marx introduced Johnny on his first appearance on *The Tonight Show*, he passed his creative torch to Johnny.

Courtesy of Stephen Cox Collection

In just the second year of the show, one of the guests was Ed Ames, who played Fess Parker's Indian sidekick Mingo on the series *Daniel Boone.* Ed was proud of the way he had learned to throw an Indian tomahawk. In a dramatic demonstration, he faced the drawing of a man on a big piece of plywood, hurled the tomahawk, and hit the man in the worst place a man could be hit if he was interested in raising a family.

And then, Johnny turned to Ed Ames and said with sweet innocence, "I didn't know you were Jewish."

That line would have been impressive enough, but Johnny was flying. He waited until the precise moment that the laughter started to recede and said, "Welcome to frontier briss."

After the cascading laughter had receded again, the embarrassed Ed Ames handed the tomahawk to Johnny, asking, "Want to try it, Johnny?"

And Johnny replied, "I couldn't hurt him any more than you did."

A triple that could only have come from him.

From the moment that Johnny took over *The Tonight Show,* I watched with awe as he pulled off savers and toppers never before seen on American TV. By our third year, audiences were almost rooting for him to bomb with a joke so they could savor Johnny's long, quizzical look and then savor an ad-lib that was even better than the dearly departed delivery.

If all else failed—and it didn't happen often—Johnny's last resorts were a rubber chicken and an arrow-through-the-head that sat on a prop table beside him, the same sort of arrow Steve Martin had used to get easy laughs. Johnny knew that if the audience ever began to sound like one that was paying its last respects, he could pick up the rubber chicken or the arrow-through-the-head and get a laugh. He hated to go fowl hunting or arrow shooting, however, because such props lowered him to the level where laughs were sought with the comic elegance of whoopee cushions, squirting flowers, and lampshades on heads.

Johnny's chicken rarely made an appearance because he had an unerring instinct for how to get a laugh. I never met a better judge of comedy or a more honest one.

One night, he began to read about six pages of jokes and it didn't take long for us to know they were going nowhere. The audience was silently informing us that it was bombs away. Suddenly, while Johnny still had a couple of pages in his hand, I picked up a lighter and set fire to them, a hot little memory from *Who Do You Trust?* My career, of course, also could have been going

From the Author's Collection

On the very first program, October 1, 1962, Johnny and I were just beginning to figure out how to follow his fundamental philosophy for the show: "Don't make it feel too planned" and "Just entertain the hell out of them."

up in smoke. Johnny gave me one of his great long takes with his steely blue eyes and then grinned and said, à la Laurel and Hardy, "You're absolutely right." And then he threw the burning pages into the wastebasket while Doc Severinsen played *Taps.* There is no script for a moment like that.

One night, in another burst of either courage or madness, I became more than a second banana—I became a champion's second. That night, Johnny's monologue was a tribute to the Eighth Air Force's impressive low-level bombing. Johnny almost always had the unique ability to be funny about not being funny, to make good jokes about his bad ones, but not on this particular night.

I had done some bombing on my own, but tried to avoid it on the show. And so, unable to watch Johnny hunting for his first laugh and afraid he was about to break out in flop sweat, I suddenly walked over to him, grabbed him by the shoulders, and spun him around to face me. Never before had I walked into that forbidden zone where Johnny did his monologue on a star carved into the floor. But now I had to revive the star who was standing on it—and falling fast. I felt like a football coach trying to stiffen the spine of one of his men.

"Now listen to me, Johnny Carson!" I said. "Don't let this audience get to you! It's time they learned why they're sitting out there and you're standing up here. You're *funnier* than they are! Even with the worst jokes, the ones you've been telling, you're still the best, so now let it fly! Go back in there and get it done."

I was telling him to win this one for our alma mater, NBC. To win one for the Gipper, even though the Gipper didn't work there. And then, just in case he hadn't been paying attention, I gave him a bracing slap on the face.

"Thanks! I needed that!" said Johnny as the audience roared.

"*Now* you're with me," Johnny said to them. "I have to get beaten up to amuse you. I was just beginning to think that you're the kind of people who would give condoms to pandas—but now I'll take that back. You're the kind of people who would give sex advice to rabbits."

The slapping of the star might not be funny today, but I did it in a time when there was a commercial for shaving lotion in which a gorgeous blonde gave a man a bracing slap on the face and he said, "Thanks! I needed that!"

It was lucky for me that, in this little play off a shaving commercial, I didn't cut my own throat.

Back into the Cave

People often ask me, "What was the funniest breakdown of a sketch on the show?" (Well, not that often. I think a guy in Toledo may have asked it, but I might have him confused with someone else.)

At any rate, there was one breakdown of a sketch that I will never forget, although I've tried to. In that sketch, Johnny was playing the oldest man in the world. Wearing a loincloth, with his hair askew, and carrying a club, he came out of a cave, where I greeted him. I had a clipboard in my hand and I was wearing a trench coat. Don't ask me why. Don't ask me why we did the whole sketch.

"I am standing here next to the oldest man in the world," I said.

"Who's that?" asked Johnny.

"That's you."

"Whatever."

"So tell me, Oldest Man in the World . . ."

"My name is Mort."

"Say, Mort, it just struck me . . ."

"Something should."

"If you have a name, it must've been given to you by your father, who must have been older than you."

"Yes, fathers usually are."

"So you're not the oldest man in the world."

"And you're not the best announcer in the world, or even in Burbank."

"Tell me, Mort, did you know the Flintstones?"

"I think I met them once at temple."

Well, *temple* was an appropriate reference because the studio audience sounded as if they were attending a memorial service. Johnny and I not only had entered the dumper, we had taken permanent residence there. Aware of this, perhaps because we were still awaiting our first laugh, Johnny suddenly turned and began walking away.

"Where are you going?" I asked.

"I'm going to get out of this sketch," he said, and he went back into the cave.

"Take me with you!" I cried and joined him in going from the dumper into the cave.

Johnny could have walked instead to his desk, beside which the small table always had those two small dumper-blockers—the rubber chicken and the arrow-through-the-head. However, because of his remarkable talent, that emergency hokeyness was almost never used. If you need a rubber chicken to get laughs, then your goose is cooked.

SWIT VS. SHARK

The best example I can remember of the two of us making a suit from whole cloth came on the night that Johnny said he had just learned something astounding about a small bird called the swit.

"I just saw a *National Geographic* show about the swit, and it's absolutely astounding," he said. "Are you aware that for the first three years of its life, the swit never stops flying? I mean, talk about your frequent fliers. This crazy bird eats in the air and mates in the air and has its babies in the air and—well, isn't that *incredible*?"

"That's fascinating," I said, "but what about the shark?"

"The shark?" he replied. "What are you talking about?"

"Well, maybe the swit bird flies all the time, but eventually it lands somewhere and says, 'Thank goodness that's over; from now

From the Author's Collection

The guests on the first *Tonight Show* included not only Groucho Marx and Rudy Vallee, but also Tony Bennett (barely visible behind me) and Joan Crawford, smiling because she must be watching herself on the monitor.

on, it's Amtrak for me,' but the shark never stops swimming. The water has to flow in and out of its gills, and if it stops swimming, it stops breathing and dies. So the swit is like a shark, only not really."

"No, All Wet One," Johnny said, "*not* just like a shark. The shark isn't flying continuously for three years. You don't have to be Peter Benchley to know that. Or even Peter Rabbit. You mean to tell me that at night the shark doesn't stop and rest?"

"Now let me ask you: How would a shark know night from day?" I said. "Or, to put it another way, day from night? But there *is* a parallel, O Learned Ornithologist."

"No, not a parallel or even a hexagon," said Johnny, sending me his usual telepathic message that we should keep rolling as long as we could. "The bird can't float—unless the birdbath is full of gin."

"A Gordon bird."

"That very species."

"But much as I hate to correct you, O Birdman of NBC, O Prime Time Peacock, the continuous swimming of the shark *is* analogous to the continuous flight of the bird."

Johnny paused and smiled at me as if to ask, *How much longer can we do this crap before they replace us with* The Three Stooges*?*

"No, Large Land Creature," he said, "it is *not* analogous, whatever that means. It is easier to swim than to fly, except on Delta. The shark can actually stop swimming and do the dead man's float in memory of his lunch."

For another few seconds, Johnny and I rolled on and the laughs did too. He had said that he never wanted the show to feel too planned, and he certainly was getting his wish with this funny free fall in which neither of us had the slightest idea of where we were going—but how happy we were to be going there.

People often thought that from time to time, Johnny deliberately structured the monologue to bomb.

"They think I want to go down the toilet," he told me. "But we work from the morning papers and sometimes the audience isn't yet aware of what's happened in the news. I guess I should base more jokes on the lottery numbers."

Every morning over coffee, Johnny would go through the paper, marking stories that might be grist for the monologue. *The Tonight Show* both shaped and reflected American opinion because Johnny began every day making circles with a pencil. And he wasn't picking horses.

nine

"Yes, Nice to Meet You, Skitch"

Although *The Tonight Show* made Johnny's attempt at privacy impossible, it took a little longer for me to become well known.

My evenings with Johnny were usually all male, either the two of us quietly alone or with other men in whose company Johnny felt relaxed. During the fall of 1963, however, shortly after Johnny's painful divorce from his childhood sweetheart and mother of his three sons, there was a brief but memorable variation of this routine. That fall, after his first full year with *The Tonight Show,* Johnny was famous, but his time as Mr. Late-Night Television was still far in the future, just as was my own time as Mr. Second Banana, a title for which there was considerably less competition.

One October night, after taping the show, we went to Sardi's, where I soon noticed a pretty young woman smiling at Johnny.

Politely, he returned the smile, the one that was already keeping millions from going to sleep. Through the years, I had noticed that women often were drawn to Johnny, but only the ones who for some reason found appeal in talent, looks, and charm.

This particular girl was pretty in a wholesome way, like Miss Sunflower at the Nebraska State Fair, where Johnny had once displayed his card tricks. With sandy blonde hair and cheeks that looked like Delicious apples, she was straight out of a Norman Rockwell picture.

"She looks like a cheerleader," I told Johnny.

"Gimme a *T*," he said. "For trouble."

"I think she'd like to meet you."

"Ed, you know I don't do that kind of thing. I haven't done it since I tried to score at college and was called for interference."

"You're doing a monologue now?" I asked and he laughed. "Johnny, she looks like a college girl. It might be fun just to talk to her."

"Well . . . I have been wondering just how much of your company I can take," he said.

"Good point, Johnny. Go talk to her."

He paused thoughtfully for a few seconds and then said, "No, I can't do that and you know why."

"All right, I'll ask her for you."

"You'd do that?" he asked.

"It won't be the first time I've introduced you."

"You don't have to say 'Heeeeere's Johnny! Just see if she wants to have a drink with us—but just *one* drink. You'll be my chaperone or else the *Enquirer* will say 'Carson Has Sex Romp à la Carte.'"

Courtesy of Stephen Cox Collection

Two grown men, graduates of major universities, at their first broadcast of *The Tonight Show* in 1962.

"It's perfectly innocent," I said.

"That's what Eve said when she had that McIntosh."

Happy that Johnny was able to unwind this way, I got up and went over to the smiling young woman.

"Pardon me, miss," I said, "but Mr. Carson is wondering if you'd like to have a drink with him."

"I'd love to," she replied.

What a surprise.

Her name was Linda; and she proved to be as charming as Johnny. I felt transported back to a dance at Sigma Chi.

"Please don't get the wrong idea from this, Mr. Carson," she said.

Courtesy of Stephen Cox Collection

When Johnny started on *The Tonight Show*, he inherited Skitch Henderson (center) from Jack Parr.

"Wrong ideas can be nice," said Johnny, " but no, Linda, I know you're here just as a fan. You *are* a fan, aren't you?"

"Yes, I love *The Tonight Show.*"

"Ed is on it too," Johnny graciously said.

"Yes, I've seen him."

I would have to find another president for my fan club.

"We'll have to make this kind of short," Johnny told her, "because . . . well, you understand."

"Oh, I certainly do. I can't believe you asked me over!"

She couldn't wait to tell all the kids at the malt shop.

"Where are you from?" he asked.

"Bakersfield," she replied.

"So you're from Bakersfield," Johnny said, as if introducing someone who had brought a collection of dancing mice.

"Well, just outside," said Linda.

Which, I sensed, was a good place to be.

"I once did stand-up in Bakersfield," said Johnny. "It wasn't a pretty sight."

And then, Linda's eyes darted to Sardi's door and she began waving at a young man who was coming in.

"That's my date!" she said, signaling the young man to come to our table. "That's Stan. He'll be thrilled to meet you."

A moment later, Stan reached us and Linda cried, "Stan, this is . . ."

"I know!" he said with a big smile. "You sure you still want to go out with me?"

And gesturing to me, she said, "And this is Skitch."

"Almost," I said, offering my hand to Stan. "Ed McMahon."

"Oh, Ed!" said Linda. "Of course it's Ed!"

"I knew that," said Johnny as Linda got up.

"Have a good time, kids," Johnny warmly said.

"Thank you both!" said Linda. "I'll never forget this!"

Yes, she would always remember her drink with Johnny and Skitch. Or was it Jack and Hugh?

ten

On a Wing and a Prayer

From the very start of the show, Johnny and I had not just a rapport but a comic rhythm. He brought out things in me that I didn't know were there, certainly not when I was doing Philadelphia's news or when I was calling to strollers on the Atlantic City boardwalk, telling them how to slice a tomato:

"Step right up, folks, and prepare to be dazzled by the world-famous Morris Metric Slicer!"

"I never heard of it, mister. Are you Morris?"

"No, I'm Ed, and I'm your new friend because you can *forget* about the two dollars these babies usually sell for! We're cutting the price to one dollar!"

"You got something for toenails?"

"You'll forget you have toes when I slice this tomato! Now tell me: What do they call New Jersey?"

"The pits."

"Yes, and also the Garden State with the world's greatest tomatoes. Now just look at this! The Morris Metric Slicer can slice a tomato so thin that you can read a newspaper through it! Use your tomato to find out the latest mayor to go to jail!"

My work as a pitchman taught me how to sell anything to anyone. My work with Johnny put me on a level I never dreamed of achieving. I am not a professional comedian or even an amateur, but there were times when Johnny made me one. A part of the show that he and I particularly loved was the few minutes after the monologue, when we improvised in what we called "the five spot." No script, no rehearsal, just the two of us in comic flight together, flying without a net. Sometimes we flew, sometimes we crashed.

Getty Images

"You dont' have to find my 'Good evening' funny, Ed."

But our altitude was usually high because we could read each other. Just a knowing look, a half smile, a certain slight movement of the head, and the signal was sent. There were nights after Johnny's monologue when he and I were ad-libbing and he seemed to have a resistance to bringing out the first guest. Seeing something in Johnny's eyes, I knew that he wanted us to go on rapping together, playing back and forth and getting wilder and wilder, until perhaps the first guest had gone home and it was time for the first commercial. I believe in ESP because Johnny and I had it. Or, as a basketball star once said after Johnny had asked how he always knew the location of a player he was feeding, "We have ESPN."

Johnny did use writers for the monologue and the sketches, but we always felt the show was best when the two of us were ad-libbing our way into the wild blue yonder.

The Leonard Bernstein of Comedy

One stunning part of Johnny's talent was that no matter how wild the show got, he always had total control. The pies flying, the chimps romping, the kids blabbing, the models flaunting their chests—all of it was grandly orchestrated by the Leonard Bernstein of comedy.

On many nights, I remembered Johnny's words, ones that could have been called the philosophy of *The Tonight Show*: "I never want the show to feel too planned."

The show certainly wasn't too planned the night that Bob Newhart and I turned back the clock—again and again. Our inspiration wasn't Albert Einstein but an author of a new book called something like *Myth and Metaphor in Modern Mexican Plumbing* or *An Anecdotal History of Wool*—one of those books that can help you fall asleep. Like many authors whose books are less than riveting, this man came out in the last ten minutes of the show and at once revealed himself to be as interesting as the directions on a tube of Vaseline. Bob and I saw that Johnny couldn't wait for these last ten minutes to pass; eagerly, his eyes kept glancing to the glassless clock at the end of the couch.

I don't remember which of us did it first, but either Bob or I was suddenly possessed to convert the show to dullness savings time. When Johnny wasn't looking, one of us moved the clock back about seven minutes. Moments later, Johnny glanced at the clock and was dismayed to see that this author's anesthetic had another seven minutes to be inhaled.

Miraculously, Johnny kept the interview on life support. And about two or three minutes later, when he wasn't looking, one of the evil twins again moved back the clock's minute hand, making it still seven minutes to the end of the show. In all the years I was with him, I had never known Johnny to panic, but he seemed to be considering it when he glanced again at the clock and saw that this deadly interview still had seven minutes to go.

Revealing how compassionate we were, Bob and I finally allowed the time to run out. Thousands of people told Johnny that he put them to sleep when they meant that he merrily kept them awake. This night, however, many people undoubtedly were put to sleep, not by Johnny, of course, but by an author who seemed to be talking for forty-five minutes.

To the Rescue!

It was wonderful to see Johnny riding to the rescue of a dying sketch.

"I took my car to the garage," he once said as a character in a sketch, "and they told me the engine was knocking."

"So they told you the engine was knocking," I said, as if taking a hearing test.

"I believe I just said precisely that," Johnny replied, "and not Hamlet's soliloquy, which, of course, might be funnier than where this is heading."

"Then let us see, O Giver of Fair Warning. When they told you the engine was knocking, what did you say?"

"I said, 'Answer it.'"

It was an ancient joke that no longer worked for third graders. When the audience didn't answer Johnny's "Answer it" with a laugh, he and I moved into gear.

"So that's what you said, did you?" I said, quoting from *The Second Banana's Handbook.*

"No, I said Lincoln's Gettysburg Address," said Johnny to just a bit of laughter. "Gee, I thought that was a joke. I seem to be alone in that thought. Forget the Gettysburg Address; it's time for prayer. Or else time to get the net."

"Perhaps I could tell a cute story about one of my children," I said.

"And clean the place out like a fire drill? Actually, I have one: Ed's baby just learned to crawl by watching Ed come into the house."

"Little Gordon."

"Yes, little Gordon."

After another moment of silence, Johnny said, "This audience isn't really bad when they're awake. Now last night . . . last night, we had a rough audience."

And from throughout the congregation came the cry, "How rough was it?"

Johnny's own net had caught them again.

The Great Zoological Debate

We also were happy going into another intellectual dead end, a zoological one, where we managed to linger for many years. Charles Darwin would have liked the long-running debate between Johnny and myself over which was smarter, the horse or the pig. Well, maybe not Charles Darwin, but certainly Charles Schulz.

Johnny thought the pig was smarter than the horse and I agreed; but the good second banana had to take the second beast.

"The pig is definitely smarter," Johnny kept telling me, resisting the temptation to discuss the future of the World Monetary Fund.

"No," I said, "if the pig were really smart, he wouldn't end up as breakfast. I mean, no one orders horse and eggs."

"Ed, I'm not aware of any pig that has become Krazy Glue. Or even the sane kind."

"Johnny, is there a Kentucky Derby for pigs? Not even a pig Pimlico. No one was ever out money on a pig. No one ever *rooted* for a pig, except another pig. It just sits there all day—in mud."

It wasn't easy for two grown men to sustain such an idiotic argument for several years, but Johnny and I were up to it—or down to it, if you prefer.

"And *pig* spelled backward is *gip*," I once said.

"That may be true, O Mascot of the Betty Ford Clinic," Johnny said. "However, pigs happen to be *architects*. Did you ever hear of any story about three little horses building a house of bricks?"

"Did you ever hear of a pig paying off at twenty to one?"

"I wonder if I should start calling you Mister Ed," he said.

"Johnny, horses have had Secretariat and Whirlaway and Seabiscuit. Name one famous pig."

"Imelda Marcos," he said.

Courtesy of Stephen Cox Collection

Carnac the Magnificent and I were both wondering if we would be replaced by a professional act.

Carnac the Magnificent

I loved ad-libbing for the five spot, but I had a special feeling for Carnac the Magnificent, the all-knowing soothsayer from the East with a massive turban who gave questions to the answers I told him. In fact, I kept padding my introduction. I think I peaked on the night that I said,

> And now, bow your heads toward Tibet—and if you don't know where Tibet is, try Pismo Beach—for here he is; that famous sage, soothsayer, and seersucker from the mysterious East; the all-knowing, all-telling, semi-omniscient dress designer to Janet Reno; the borderline sage, would-be prophet, and Nepalese underachiever . . . *Carnac the Magnificent!*

And out came Johnny in his oversized robe and preposterous headdress—the towering bejeweled turban that belonged on a seven-foot center. He started walking toward the desk, missed a step, and grandly fell on his face.

On that particular night, I not only enriched my introduction, but I was able to turn Carnac into heartwarming payback to Johnny for what he had done to me a few weeks before by letting me twist in the wind during an Aunt Blabby sketch.

"Welcome, O Great Sage," I said.

"May a thousand blessings flow across your body," Johnny said.

"That many, O Magnificent One?"

"With *that* body, a thousand might not be enough. May you get your first French kiss from a diseased camel. May a love-starved fruit fly molest your sister's nectarines."

"Abuse from you is like praise from anyone else," I said.

"I don't know what that means, but I know everything else."

"And now the envelope with the answer to the unknown question," I said, holding it in the air. "I have in my hand, as you can plainly see . . ."

"Of *course* I can plainly see, and unfortunately I'm seeing you."

"I said those particular words, O Semidivine One, because sometimes the sand gets in your eyes and . . ."

"May sand fleas get in your shorts."

"Back to the envelope. A child of six could plainly see that it is hermetically sealed."

"What's that child doing up at midnight?"

"That is not one of your questions, O Semisplendid One. Let me return to the valid questions and say that *my daughter*, who is four and a half but acts considerably older, can plainly see that the question has been kept in a mayonnaise jar on Funk and Wagnalls's porch since noon. *No* one, absolutely *no* one—" And I pounded the desk.

"Carnac may have to call security."

"—knows its contents!"

"You are right, Large Person," said Johnny. "May those blessings keep flowing over you, with some Gordon's as well."

"O Source of All That Is Wet, O Divine Spigot, we are ready for your first intuition."

"May we have absolute silence, please," he said.

"Many times you have received that," I said, triggering a huge laugh with perhaps the best zinger I had ever thrown on the show.

After letting the laugh play, Johnny said, "Clearly, you have funds put away."

Carnac the Magnificent

Of all the routines that Johnny and I did, our favorite was Carnac the Magnificent, who gave new meaning to the word *magnificent*. He was a sage from the mysterious East, which was mysterious to him because he didn't know where it was. He didn't know much else either. In fact, the totality of his wisdom is in these thirty questions and answers. The answers always came first. Backwards was Carnac's style.

Answers

"Silence Please . . ."

1. Moonies
2. A cat and your wife
3. Lollipop
4. Preparation H and take-home pay
5. Dairy Queen
6. The American people
7. Sis Boom Bah
8. A B C D E F G
9. Mr. Coffee
10. The Loch Ness Monster
11. Mount Baldy
12. The zip code
13. A linen closet
14. 20/20
15. "Thank you, PaineWebber"
16. Coal Miner's Daughter
17. Real people
18. NAACP, FBI, IRS
19. I give a damn
20. Hasbro
21. Spam and Jim Bakker
22. Ovaltine
23. Bungy diving and a date with Geraldo
24. Hop Sing
25. All systems go
26. 10–4
27. Persnickety
28. "These are a few of my favorite things"
29. Hell or high water

Announcer: "I hold in my hand . . . the last envelope."

30. A pair of Jordache jeans and a bread box

Carnac's Questions

1. Name a religion that drops its pants.
2. Name something you put out at night and someone who won't.
3. What happens when someone stomps on your lolly?
4. What can you depend on for shrinking?
5. What do you call a gay milkman?
6. Name the loser in the 1976 presidential race.
7. Describe the sound made when a sheep explodes.
8. What were some of the earlier forms of Preparation H?
9. Name the father of Mrs. Olsen's illegitimate baby.
10. Who will they find sooner than Jimmy Hoffa?
11. How do you play piggyback with Telly Savalas?
12. What do CIA agents have to remember to go to the bathroom?
13. What do gay Irish guys come out of?
14. What will a gallon of gas cost by next year?
15. What might a girl say at a stockbrokers' orgy?
16. Where can you pick up a nasty soot-rash?
17. What do lonely inflatable people buy for companionship?
18. How do you spell naacpfbiirs?
19. What did it say in the beaver's will?
20. How does Tito Jackson get work?
21. Name two things that'll be in the can for the next eighteen years.
22. Describe Oprah Winfrey in high school.
23. Name two things that end with a jerk on your leg.
24. Name a prison for one-legged people.
25. What happens if you take a Sinutab, a Maalox, and a Feen-a-Mint?
26. How do a big guy and a little guy split fourteen bucks?
27. How do you get paid when you're picking snicketies?
28. What do you say to a doctor who's wearing a rubber glove?
29. Name two things you really don't want in your underwear.
30. Name two places where you stuff your buns.

Handing him the envelope, I finally said, "And now, O Great Wind from the East, here is the answer to your first question."

"I was afraid we'd never get to this," Johnny said. "And I was afraid we *would.*"

He pressed the envelope to his forehead and said, "V-8."

"V-8," I said, and Johnny eloquently scowled at me.

And then he opened the envelope and read, "What kind of social disease can you get from an octopus?"

The audience laughed and then groaned.

"This audience would lob a grenade at Bambi's mother," Johnny said.

From the Author's Collection

This picture says it all. It shows the joy of my thirty-four years working with Johnny and the love we had for each other. We were a big Irishman and a slim WASP, but brothers to the core.

Carroll Seghers/Globe Photos

What a delicious irony that at the end of every one of Johnny's monologues was a swing from a game that he had abandoned after depositing his clubs in a Florida lake.

Globe Photos, Inc.

Whether he was Rambo, Turbo, or Carnac, somehow you always knew it was Johnny.

Bill Crespinel/Globe Photos

NBC/Globe Photos

Johnny's first appearance in front of the curtain after the show had moved to Burbank. the name *Burbank* became a running gag, especially the part of it that was "beautiful downtown Burbank."

Courtesy of Stephen Cox Collection

Courtesy of Stephen Cox Collection

We had more fun than the Three Stooges and never threw a thing at each other, unless you count those eggs.

Courtesy of Stephen Cox Collection

The twenty-fifth anniversary of *The Tonight Show* was the biggest celebration we had had up to that point. And our hair was turning a color fitting for the silver anniversary.

Supplied by NBC-Globe Photos

Two good friends, forever on the same frequency.

Supplied by NBC/Globe Photos, Inc.

All good things must come to an end. But in our case there will be DVDs to watch forever. The last *Tonight Show* was on May 22, 1992.

Associated Press, AP

Associated Press, AP; Associated Press, AP

eleven

On the Road to Euphoria

One night, after one of Johnny's jokes bombed, I jumped in to act as a kind of cheerleader.

"I'm bewildered by the lack of appreciation," I said. "That seemed funny to me."

"I hate to see you so lonely, Ed," Johnny said.

"Well, that was definitely a joke."

"You know," he said, "when I do a joke, you don't have to be master of ceremonies and say, 'Hey, how about *that*!'"

"I do tonight," I said and the two of us exploded with laughter.

"I need a meeting with my writers," Johnny said.

"Were they here today?" I asked.

"Yes, and I wish I'd seen them."

And then, to the audience, he said, "You like to see me struggle, don't you?"

They did like to see him struggle because they knew he was gifted enough to always turn defeat into victory and they delighted in seeing him do it. So did I because he was able to bring new gems out of the ashes.

When a baby marmoset found a home on Johnny's head, he said, "I look like Fess Parker."

"He obviously likes gray," I said.

"I doubt he'd like being on you, Ed," Johnny said, "unless he likes the smell of olives." And then, to America, he said, "I don't want to say that Ed drank a lot last night, but this morning the AAA had to attach jumper cables to start his liver."

Oops!

Although selective zingers from me did work, I always knew my place on the show, especially after one painful moment in our New York days. Johnny had been demonstrating an anti-mosquito spray. Just before using it, he said, "I hear that mosquitoes go only for really passionate people."

Almost by reflex, I said, "There's another one!" and slapped my wrist, wrecking Johnny's gag. I should have known never to go where he was going.

With a cold smile, Johnny reached below his desk, picked up a giant can of insect spray, and said, "I guess I won't be needing this prop, will I?"

During the next commercial break, I said, "I'm really sorry I did that."

"That's okay, Ed," he replied. "You'll be able to do that all you want in your new job at Bayonne Chevrolet."

Such a slip, of course, was rare. Most of the time on the show, I knew when to talk and when to keep quiet, even though it often was hard to keep my mouth shut. Because I'd had so many of my own shows, there were times when I had to stop myself from responding to something Johnny said, especially at those rare moments when I thought of the same ad-lib. Being his sidekick was a challenging role. I had to help him but never get in his way, to be in there when I was needed but step back when I wasn't, without ever looking as though I was doing anything.

NBC/Globe Photos, Inc.

"That's okay Ed. You'll be able to do that all you want in your new job at Bayonne Chevrolet."

"All you do on the show is laugh," a man from the studio once told me, and of course I had to pretend that laughing was my whole job. I had to be like the Lone Ranger. I had to be the Lone Straight Man and never talk about the good I did. Hi-yooo, Johnny!

"If Johnny got a laugh track, he wouldn't need you," a teenage girl once said to me.

"I guess I'm lucky," I replied, "that a laugh track can't sell Alpo."

"How Cold Was It?"

Most of the time, our rhythm was like the rhythm of Bob Hope and Bing Crosby in their road pictures. In a story he wrote about the show, Johnny nicely described how our radar worked. You may call this insincere self-promotion, and you would be wrong. In all our years together, Johnny never said one word to me that wasn't sincere; I don't know how he ever got into show business.

"Ed and I developed an unspoken method of communication," Johnny wrote, "the kind married couples often have. We never had a blueprint, but both of us always sensed where to go for the laughs—and we moved each other in those directions. When it was really working, it was euphoria. When it wasn't, well . . . there was always the next night."

Whether Johnny and I were headed for euphoria or euthanasia, sometimes the audience became part of our trip, such as our journey into mad meteorology. On one show during our days in New York, Johnny happened to say, "It was really cold out here today."

"How . . . cold . . . was . . . it?" I asked, as if teaching English to a Martian child.

"It was so cold," he said, "that I saw a robin put his worm in a microwave."

We did this routine so often that the audience finally started joining in, chanting, "How cold *was* it?" even when the thermometer read ninety-five.

Or "How hot *was* it?" to which Johnny would reply, "It was so hot that I saw a pigeon walking in the shadow of Orson Welles" or "It was so hot that I saw a robin dipping his worm in Nestea."

An all-weather bird, that robin.

On another night, Johnny said, "This is a strange audience."

Recognizing its cue, the audience asked, "How strange is it?"

"I'll tell you," Johnny said. "Just before the show, an elderly lady came up to me and said, 'I'd like to capture you on canvas.' And I said, 'You'd like to paint my picture?' And she said, 'No, I've got an army cot in my Winnebago.'"

That Pesky Quicksand!

The show really should have been called *Borden's Bandwagon* because Johnny and I milked everything. In our mystical way, we got laughs from the most unlikely material, often proving why it was unlikely.

One night, Johnny read a list of what a person should do if he finds himself caught in quicksand, a pesky problem for so many viewers. Don't you just *hate* it when that happens?

When Johnny had reached the end of the list, my soliloquy began.

"Johnny, everyone, and I mean *everyone,* who now happens to be in quicksand will be eternally grateful for you, especially if he gets out. I just don't know how you do it."

"Are you finished, Martini Breath?" he asked.

"*Finished?* Some of those people in quicksand may be finished,

Courtesy of Stephen Cox Collection

America's cool King of Late Night, whose nervousness about holding the throne could be seen when he kept straightening his already straight tie.

all of them perhaps, but I'm just starting to express my admiration for you!"

"Must I stay and hear it?"

"That's just *it*!" I cried. "That's what I'm trying to *say*!"

"But not very well."

"You have to leave because you're so incredibly busy, and yet you manage to find time to go to a library or dentist's office or trash can and come out with a list like that. Further words fail me."

"I pray for that."

"You are an inspiration to every American who is planning to get lost in a swamp!"

"I don't know what to say," Johnny said. "Yes, I do, Camel Mouth. May one of your sons become a Rockette."

Calendar Sense

As part of the spontaneous merriness that dominated the shows, I sometimes threw Johnny a curve; but Johnny could hit the curve as well as Ted Williams did.

One Thursday night, I said, "Johnny, I won't be here tomorrow. You'll have to do the show without me, if such a thing is possible."

"Tomorrow is Friday, Ed," he replied. "It's not the weekend. Let me teach you how to read a calendar. Or are you using the Chinese one?"

"Well," I said, "I can take a day off once in a while, can't I? You certainly invented it."

After the audience roared, Johnny said, "*Your* next invention may be unemployment."

Another time, I gave Johnny a lesson in following the calendar.

"Today is Wednesday," he said, "and on Wednesday—"

"Excuse me, Johnny," I said.

"You want to leave the room, Ed?"

"No, I don't like to correct the star, but . . ."

"Oh, yes you do. And I may find a new one for you to correct."

"I just wanted to say, in the most humble way, that today is *Thursday*. They may not have taught days of the week in Nebraska."

"Ed is right," Johnny said. "Today *is* Thursday and I thank Ed for pointing that out, even though he didn't have to. You see, folks, a good announcer and a good star go hand in hand. But not in the hallway."

Yes, with the ease of Hope and Crosby.

twelve

Tying One On

In the department of inspired silliness, Johnny and I once did a fashion show that no one had ever seen or ever will see on an American runway.

After I returned from a vacation, Johnny and I began talking about what I had done.

"So where did you go, Ed?" he asked. "I know Cincinnati is in season."

"I went to Acapulco, Johnny," I said.

"What was it like there? And feel free not to tell me."

"Well, as a matter of fact, Johnny, I studied some weird local customs."

"That's what I do in Burbank."

"I went to this one restaurant and it had the craziest custom

I've ever seen. If you're wearing a tie, they cut it off when you walk in the door."

"Sort of a silky circumcision."

"Not exactly, Johnny, because then they nail the tie to the wall and I don't think they do that in a . . ."

"No, they probably don't."

"So the whole wall of the restaurant is filled with people's ties."

"That's totally insane," he said.

"No it isn't, because once you're sitting there with just a piece of your tie, the whole tone of the evening changes."

"You feel less tied down."

"I wouldn't have said that, but you do feel totally relaxed."

"It still sounds like one of the dumbest things I've ever heard. Maybe this country should consider cutting its ties to Mexico. And if I do another bad tie joke, please tie me up," he said.

"Johnny, it was actually so much fun that—well, if I had scissors right now . . ."

At that moment, I knew if I extended my arm, the propman would put a pair of scissors in my hand—which is precisely what he did. He slapped it into my hand like a forceps for an operation.

And now, armed with my instrument, I did the only thing that a graduate of a major university could do. I reached across the desk and with the courage expected of a Marine, I cut off Johnny's tie. I put the tie down in front of him and put the scissors on top of it, wondering if the Jesuits who had taught me would have been proud.

Johnny responded like the civilized man he was. He rose, came around the desk, cut off my tie, and put it and the scissors on the coffee table before me. Proudly, like a matador having presented a bull's ear to his beloved, he returned to his desk. And Laurel and Hardy would have been proud of him too.

The curtain now went up for Act Two of *The Cutups.* In dramatic proof that I had only a tenuous connection to maturity, I reached over to Johnny and snipped off all the buttons on his shirt. There was, of course, only one sensible response for him. He came back to me and cut off the points of my collar.

The audience was going crazy. Johnny and I, of course, beat them to that destination. Some of them must have wondered what the two of us would do when we were finally nude.

After Johnny had let the crescendo of laughter play out, he told me, "I want you to know what you've done."

"I think I do," I said. "I was paying attention."

"What I mean is I've been wearing this tie for seven years."

"Well, you won't be wearing it again," I said.

And now, in spite of the continuing laughter, Johnny and I stopped our tailoring because we were aware that we had gone far enough. If we had begun cutting our suits, we would have been damaging something of greater value and showing insensitivity to some guy in South Dakota who had just lost his job and had only one suit to wear—not shred.

After recovering from the wackiness, Johnny paused, looked at me in wonder, and began the little litany we loved: "Two grown men."

And of course, I replied, "Graduates of major universities."

Three Favorites

The "two grown men who were graduates of major universities" phrase was one of our great running gags. And there were others.

Every year on *The Tonight Show*, Johnny and I did three particular jokes to which our audiences always responded. The first one came in December.

"Ed," Johnny said, "I was really devastated when I learned there was no Santa Claus."

"That can be devastating," I said. "How old were you, Johnny?"

"I was twenty-five at the time."

In the second joke, I played straight man again.

"Ed, you never forget your first sexual experience," he annually said.

"That's for sure," I replied. I could really zing those comebacks.

"How well I remember mine."

"Where was it, Johnny?" asked the Kinsey of NBC.

"In the backseat of my father's car."

"In the backseat of your father's car?"

"That's what I just said."

"Johnny, can you remember with whom you had this first sexual experience?"

"I was alone at the time."

That car, by the way, is in the Imperial Palace Museum in Las Vegas. You expected the Smithsonian?

In the third joke, Johnny asked, "Ed, did I ever tell you about a special girl in my old high school, Lincoln High?"

"Every year," I said, "but I never get tired of hearing about her because I never get tired of being employed."

"You better not, or you'll be seeing a lot of Dick Clark."

"You know, I used to live next to Dick in Philadelphia. In fact, it was Dick who was really responsible for my getting the job on . . ."

"No one's interested, Ed. Not even your wife. Let's get back to that special girl."

"Yes, we don't want to leave her."

"Her name was Jenny Satchitori and she was voted Miss Lincoln. Do you happen to know why?"

"No, Johnny. Why was Jenny Satchitori voted Miss Lincoln?"

"Because everybody took a shot at her in the balcony."

Banana Advice from Ed

For those of you interested in a career as a second banana instead of legitimate work, here's a tip you won't learn when getting your A.B. (Advanced Banana) degree: *You have to know how to ask the star precisely the right questions.*

When the star says that his first sexual experience was in the back of his father's car, you can't say, "What happened?" or "Oh, really?" or "No kidding." Those words don't lead to the payoff. You have to ask, "Can you remember with whom you had the first sexual experience?" It's not brain surgery; it's not even dermatology; but it's a minor art form that I practiced for thirty-four years with the funniest man I ever knew.

Three Private Jokes

Johnny and I also had some private jokes that came up regularly. One that still makes me smile involved the sixteenth president of the United States. From time to time, Johnny would put on a stovepipe hat, a beard, and play Abraham Lincoln in a bit that always ended up the way Lincoln did after catching that show at Ford's Theatre. Johnny always made it funny for me, however, and probably just for me. He was too subtle for most of the studio audience or the network viewers. After another Lincoln bit lay there like Lincoln in state, Johnny would turn to me and say, "Too soon."

"Yes," I would say, "too soon."

We meant, of course, that it was tasteless of us to joke about Lincoln only 120 years after he was shot.

"Too soon" was not the only private joke that Johnny and I shared. For the four years of *Who Do You Trust?* and the first three years of *The Tonight Show,* I commuted to New York from Philadelphia, where I had built my dream house. Yes, I know that W. C. Fields would have said, "If your dream house is in Philadelphia, you don't need a haunted one." But there it was, and every day I had to take a train to New York, which passed the Gordon's Gin plant in Linden, New Jersey. That plant was hardly the Statue of Liberty, but I happened to notice it, and the Statue of Liberty made nothing I drank.

During this time of my commuting, *The Tonight Show* had a bit called "The Homework School of the Air," in which Johnny gave funny answers to questions from youngsters in our audience. Well, they were *supposed* to be funny answers, and if the show had stayed on a second thirty years, one or two of them might have made it.

One day in the first year of the show, I said, "Johnny, here's a nice letter from a little boy named Gordon in Linden, New Jersey. He asks, 'Why is the sky blue?'"

"Why not?" Johnny replied. "Let him think about that, but not too long."

A few weeks later, Gordon from Linden wrote again, this time to ask why the sea was salty.

"It is?" said Johnny. "I never noticed that."

And then a third letter came from Gordon with another question Johnny couldn't answer. He should have been doing the "Every Child Left Behind School of the Air."

"That Gordon from Linden, he writes a lot, doesn't he?" asked Johnny with the smile of a man who knew what I drank.

"Yes, he's thirsty for knowledge," I said.

"Nice that he keeps in touch with us. I wonder if he knows any little foreign students in his school. Like the Smirnoff boy from Minsk or little Sherry from Marseilles."

Another running private joke came about because Johnny got upset when he read a newspaper headline about his matrimonial life, which had its ups and downs during three marriages. That all changed when he finally found the love of his life, Alexis Mass, and remained on a high with her for fourteen years. I remember a day when one of his downs was caused by a newspaper story about the alimony he was paying to his second wife. Johnny always read newspapers to feed his monologue; but every once in a while, they fed his temper. On a day like that, no one wanted to be near him—not the writers, not the producer, not the propman.

My routine at the show was always to go first to one of our two producers, either Fred de Cordova or Peter Lassally, to find out if there was anything in particular that I should know for the show that night.

"Boy, he doesn't want to see anyone today," Fred told me that morning, "except maybe a certain newspaper editor to fight a duel. They've got his alimony payment again, and it sounds like first prize in the lottery."

I *had* to see Johnny for my usual seven minutes of preparation to ad-lib, however, and the Marine Corps would have expected me to have the courage to do it. Just before I saw him, I did some calculating and figured out how much his alimony came to for each minute of the marriage. When I walked in, I gave him this figure and then asked, "Awake or asleep?"

He was silent for a moment, while I began figuring out how much per minute my severance pay would be, and then he banged his fist on his desk, said, "You no good son of a bitch!" and began to laugh.

A few hours later on the show, he turned to me and asked with a sly grin, "Awake or asleep?"

Americans must have been mystified to hear one of our three private jokes—"Too soon," "Gordon," and "Awake or asleep?" And Johnny, who never forgot anything, later threw the joke back at me. After my own alimony had been in print, he said, "Ed, I saw something about your alimony payments in today's paper."

"Oh really, Johnny."

"Awake or asleep?"

thirteen

Have Jokes, Will Travel

Johnny and I had a comic rhythm even away from the cameras. At state fairs all over the country, we used to have a two-man act in which he played a certain character that I would interview.

"And here he is, ladies and gentlemen," I would boom, "the most dramatic disproof of evolution, Mr. Art Fern!"

And Johnny would appear as the classic hick he often played on the show.

"Mr. Fern," I would ask, "what are you doing in Akron?"

"What is *anyone* doing in Akron?" he would reply. "Seeing how it feels to live on Devil's Island, I guess."

"That may be true, but—"

"That may be true? You're quick."

"What I want to say is . . ."

"But you're having trouble with the English?" Johnny asked.

". . . is do you do anything specific in Akron? Like making tires."

"No, I make tracks. I'm in the Witness Protection Program."

"You and your whole family?"

"I don't know if they're my family. The woman won't tell me her name. I think it's Corleone."

"Well, how is life in the Witness Protection Program?"

"Could be worse. I could be on the *Johnny Carson* program."

"What did you do to get here?"

For thirty-four years on TV, Johnny carried me. Once in Florida, I reversed things.

From the Author's Collection

"About five years. Then I made a deal. I turned in my mother."

"You turned in your mother?"

"What do you think I just said, the Pledge of Allegiance? At least it gave her a chance to get out of the house."

"Mr. Fern," I said, "I hope you don't mind my saying this . . ."

"I certainly do."

". . . but your name—Art Fern—is a little strange."

"Oh, I changed it."

"From what?"

"Peter Pond Scum."

Wildcat Sam

For years, all over the country, we played state fairs, where Johnny re-created some of the beloved characters from the show.

One of my favorites was an oilman named Wildcat Sam, who was about as smart as a derrick. In my reporter's trench coat, I would put a microphone before Sam's dippy face and ask, "Wildcat, what brings you to the Kansas State Fair?"

"Bad luck," he'd reply. "Of course, it could be worse. I could be in Leavenworth. No, that's actually a better crowd."

"Tell me, Wildcat," I'd say, "how is the oil flowing?"

"Want yours changed?" Johnny would say. "I usually do it only in cars, but you look a quart low. 'Course, *that* ain't the quart you want."

"No, it isn't."

"That's what I just said. Try to think of something all by yourself."

"Tell me, Wildcat, do you think the price of gas will be going up?"

"What's the price of gas got to do with oil?"

"Gas comes from oil."

"It does? I thought it came from Congress. That's a little joke."

"Very little."

"Say, Mister McMuffin—"

"McMahon."

"Close enough."

"Wildcat, did you know that Johnny Carson is from the Midwest?"

"So was Dillinger. He was Public Enemy Number One."

"I thought that was your mother."

"I'll do the jokes."

"When do you plan to start?"

King Tut

The other character that Johnny and I took from the show to state fairs was King Tut. Johnny would come out in Tut's enormous striped headdress and I would say, "King Tut, the people of Oklahoma are looking to you for wisdom."

"It seems to me," he replied, "that the people of Oklahoma are looking for their teeth."

"But you seem to have yours. You are truly a remarkable man. Tell me, are you embalmed right now?"

"You probably are."

"To be insulted by the sun god is an honor."

"Man, you're dumber than the Egyptians who thought I was the sun god. Anyone who worshiped *me* was an atheist. So this is Oklahoma, eh?"

Courtesy of Stephen Cox Collection

Johnny's King Tut was one of the characters in our act at state fairs all over the country. Tut was roughly the age of some of our jokes.

"Well, it's not the Valley of the Kings."

"Or downtown Queens."

"No, Your Magnificence, it is neither. We have no pyramids here. By the way, it was quite impressive for you to build those pyramids."

"What the hell do you think I should have built? Golden arches? A hockey rink? A freeway to Libya?"

"You're pretty cranky today."

"You'd be cranky too if you hadn't had sex for five thousand years."

"But you did have a nice romp with Queen Nefertiti," I would say to King Tut.

"Yes, but penicillin wasn't invented yet," he would reply. "And I could never pronounce her name. I never knew if Nefertiti was her first or last name, and she didn't know either."

"You're complaining a lot for a man who was king of all Egypt."

"King of all Egypt? You think I was just king of Cairo? Anyway, Egypt is nothing much to be king of. It's Cleveland with sphinx."

"Ah yes, the sphinx. How did you build it?"

"Well, it wasn't with Lincoln Logs. I used a lot of guys with no accident insurance. Luckily, they weren't Teamsters."

"Weren't you the pharaoh who dealt with Moses and got all those plagues?"

"Right! Vermin and locusts. Vermin we already had, and we had enough grasshoppers too. One of the plagues they missed was listening to this act."

fourteen

Here Comes the Rating!

In the fall of 1969, the name Tiny Tim would have meant only a kid in *A Christmas Carol* had Johnny not introduced to America the improbable long-haired, ukulele-playing, falsetto-voiced hippie whose endearing bizarreness had first charmed America on *Laugh-In*. And, as you may remember, Tiny Tim was married on *The Tonight Show*—a wedding that got the biggest audience in the history of the show. Ironically, Tiny Tim had auditioned for *Who Do You Trust?* and had been rejected by Art Stark, perhaps because not too many men were wearing lipstick in 1959.

Accompanying himself on the ukulele, Tim used to sing not only "Tiptoe Through the Tulips," but also a song that was a lyrical request for medical help:

I gotta see a doctor,
I gotta see a doctor,
'Cause there's something wrong with me.
What can it be?

A Wedding to Remember

If ever a man begged the question, Tiny Tim did in that song. There is, of course, something wrong with all of us. However, Tiny Tim seemed to have gotten an extra share.

Or had he? Was is all just a clever act? Like most people, I never knew if Tim was bizarre just on the surface or if he was a fruitcake at the core. Was the *real* Tiny Tim a man who had his mother's voice and hair? Perhaps when he went home, he bacame Herbert Khaury again, his voice dropped an octave, and he thought, *I gotta find a new act where I don't have to look and sound like Madame Butterfly.*

It all began casually. One night late in '69 when Tiny Tim was on the show, Johnny asked him, "Is there a girl in your life?"

Tiny Tim began to giggle.

Raising his pencil, Johnny said, "I'll mark that as a yes."

And then Tiny Tim began talking about Miss Vicki, who was so wonderful that he had fallen in love with her and would never tiptoe through the tulips with anyone else.

"So does that mean you're getting married?" asked Johnny.

"Oh, yes!" said Tim in a voice slightly higher than Miss Vicky's.

"Well," said Johnny, "you'll get married on the show."

It was an offhanded remark, but it turned into something that belonged on the cover of *Modern Bride.*

And lo, it came to pass that Tiny Tim and Miss Vicki Budinger were married that December in the Church of Carson by a real minister, who may have been defrocked immediately afterward.

The wedding ceremony itself, for which 268 studio tickets were given to guests of the bride and groom, should have been nullified by the groom's first words: "I, Tiny Tim, being of sound mind . . ."

Instead, all of us onstage were in black tie, while Miss Vicki sat demurely beside me on the couch, her one hand clutching one of Tim's and her other clutching the bridal bouquet. She should have been tossing it to some single young woman who would then have a souvenir of a marriage that might have made Freud want to switch to pediatrics.

NBC/Globe Photos, Inc.

The wedding of Tiny Tim and Miss Vicki was America's second-highest-rated television event, behind only the Super Bowl.

When Tiny Tim and Miss Vicki got married, it was an event that made Tim "so happy" until six months later when they parted ways.

Courtesy of Stephen Cox Collection

Miss Vicki should have suspected that her husband wasn't headed for a white picket fence but perhaps white-coated men when he sang:

Oh won't you come and love me, oh pretty Vicki mine?
Oh, won't you come and love me and be my valentine?
Like violets and roses, our spirits will entwine.
Like violets and roses, our bodies will entwine.

Miss Vicki wasn't to spend very long in that garden; Tiny Tim divorced her in less than a year.

After the ceremony, Tim prepared milk and honey for a toast, but milk and honey never did much for Johnny and me. They made a lousy martini.

"Gordon," I whispered to Johnny. "For that little boy."

"Even better," he said, opening a bottle of champagne. "For those two grown men."

"Graduates of major universities."

Johnny did respect marriage—four times, in fact—and he did not play Tiny Tim's wedding for laughs. With his usual good taste, Johnny didn't let the show mock Tiny Tim in any way. He must have done it the right way because the show became America's second-highest-rated television event, behind only the Super Bowl: More than twenty-one million people watched Tiny Tim and Miss Vicki march through the white canopy on our stage and over to Johnny and me at the desk, while Wagner's "Wedding March" was played.

After the wedding, in keeping with the absurd nature of the whole NBC event, there was a reception on the ground floor of the CBS Building. The happy couple, however, missed the trifecta by not spending their wedding night in a green room at ABC.

At the reception, Tiny Tim came up to me and said, "Oh, Mr. McMahon, I'm so happy!"

"That's nice, Tim," I said.

"And I was so honored that you came to my wedding."

I didn't want to deflate him by saying that I worked in the chapel. "Well, Tim," I said, wondering if the solemnity of the occasion called for my calling him Mr. Tim. "It's an event I will never forget."

I also will never forget *The Wizard of Oz.*

fifteen

Westward, Hi-Yooo!

Johnny was the greatest perfectionist I have ever known. Near the end of any show that he felt had not been excellent, he would say to me during a commercial, "Well, there's always tomorrow."

At other times during a commercial, he would become a TV critic and ask, "How much longer do you think we can get away with this?"

One night, during a commercial that followed a stillborn sketch, Johnny made my favorite off-air remark.

"Ed," he said, "do you know my dream? I really want to become an aluminum siding salesman."

The commercial just after the five spot was when Johnny often talked to me, sometimes dropping a bombshell. One night around 1970, he softly said, "You know, why don't we move the show to California?"

"A great idea," I said. "We'd have the best guests out there."

"More important, the best weather for tennis."

When *The Tonight Show* started, New York was the center of the entertainment industry. Rudy Tellez, an early producer of the show, remembers Johnny saying, "I'm never leaving New York. I love it." But in the early seventies, Fred de Cordova—Mr. Hollywood—had become the producer and wanted the show moved to California; more celebrities were available in California, and Johnny was enduring a bitter divorce struggle in New York. Johnny explained that "there's not much television in New York anymore. When you do five shows every week for a year, it's a little sticky sometimes to find a large number of lively people in New York."

Time Life Pictures/Getty Images

Johnny and myself with our masterful producer, Fred De Cordova, at a 1992 Communications Award ceremony honoring Johnny. A former film producer, Fred brought a disciplined intelligence to *The Tonight Show*.

And so in 1972 we moved to Burbank.

In Burbank, *The Tonight Show* aired from the studio that Bob Hope had used, and one Johnny liked. When we did the show in New York, we had used a converted radio studio that had only 250 seats. It was very small.

How small was it?

It was so small that when Dodge once demanded I use a real car in a commercial, we had to cut one in half and use only the front half; but the Burbank studio could fit a stretch limo. Johnny liked a big studio, and this one was so big that when he played the Jolly Green Giant, huge kernels of corn were able to fall as a sight gag. There were nights when I was expecting the arrival of other vegetables as well.

Bob Hope had insisted that the seats in that studio be steeply banked so the last row could be as close as possible and the laughs from it would be coming to him at the same time as those from the front. Johnny also wanted the audience to react as one unit, and not send him laughs in installments.

The audience certainly reacted as one unit when an elderly lady named Myrtle Young brought to Johnny her prize collection of potato chips, which had remarkable shapes. She had made the crispy shapes of such things as a beagle, a flower, and a candle.

Glancing at Johnny, I said, "Look at this one."

"Oh yes," she said, "it's Yogi Bear."

"Can't these break?" I asked.

"They certainly can," she said; and while she spoke to me with her eyes away from Johnny, he reached into a bowl of potato chips and chomped on one with the unmistakable sound of a chomped potato chip.

Myrtle Young looked at him as if she were seeing a Hitchcock film and she clutched her heart.

"I don't think the nurse is on duty now," I said, and then Johnny allowed her to breathe again by revealing that he had eaten a chip that belonged in no one's collection. It was the kind of lovably impish thing he could spontaneously do better than anyone else.

Johnny connected well not just with people of all ages and eccentricities, but also with other species, like the animals that Joan Embrey brought from the San Diego Zoo to the show: the gibbon, the goat, the baby kangaroo, the baby ape, the mar-

Johnny connected well not just with people, but also with other species, like the animals that Joan Embrey brought from the San Diego Zoo. Is the chimp holding a pencil to ease his nerves as Johnny did? Or does he have a new gag?

Courtesy of Stephen Cox Collection

moset, and the chimpanzee. Johnny loved turning the show into his own Wild Kingdom, which inspired the wildness that often burst from him.

I've mentioned the unforgettable night when one of Joan Embrey's baby leopards growled at Johnny and he decided to say good-bye to it, sprinted across the stage, and jumped into my arms. A hilarious moment, and so was the moment when one of Joan's chimps preferred hugging Johnny to eating a banana. When I tried to pet the chimp, he pulled away. He wanted nothing to do with a second banana either.

Yes, the timing of Johnny's reactions was always flawless: the sly grins and the long deadpan double takes that he learned from Jack Benny. I will never forget the look on Johnny's face when one of Joan Embrey's marmosets climbed up to his head and just sat there. He seemed to have been born knowing the funniest possible responses, both physical and verbal, to suddenly wearing a furry headpiece.

"Tell me one other place in this whole world of seven billion people," he said, "where a man is sitting with a marmoset on his head."

The Take-No-Prisoners Gene

Whether in New York or California, this seemingly laid-back Nebraska boy drove himself like a Prussian general. In every enterprise, he was both a perfectionist and a fierce competitor. Not only did he want his show to be the very best, but he wanted to be the very best at every other activity too. It was a take-no-prisoners gene that came directly from his mother, an inheritance I discovered when he asked his parents to play poker with us.

After Johnny and I had played a state fair anywhere near his home, he invited his mother and father to come back to his hotel, and he didn't want to look at baby pictures; he wanted to play killer poker. Johnny's father was a gentle man, but his mother was a killer at cards; and so, she and Johnny played not like a Hallmark mother and son but like Mother Earp and Wyatt.

When Johnny made his memorable three jokes after Ed Ames had thrown his tomahawk at the most tender part of the target, Johnny let the laugh play and then he sharpened the tomahawk, eager to show how well *he* could throw it.

In everything Johnny did, he felt a compulsion to excel, a truth I learned one night at a cocktail party in Omaha, where I met people with past connections to him. One of the girls had dated him, one of the guys had boxed with him—and he wanted to be a knockout with both. When he went to Russia, he learned Russian; when he went to Africa, he learned Swahili. Some TV stars are still working on English.

As you know, Johnny finished every *Tonight Show* monologue with an easy golf swing. What delicious irony! On a vacation in Fort Lauderdale in November of 1962, after the show had been on the air for just a few weeks, Johnny played a round of golf at a country club the way so many people play—he stank. Luckily, however, while feeling his mind beginning to depart, he found relief at a water hole. He threw his clubs into it and was happy to see them disappear because it wasn't a water hole, it was a lake.

Now aware that golf was a gift to man from Satan, Johnny vowed never to play again. The following day, he took up tennis;

and because of his passion to excel, he didn't merely *play* tennis, he strove for excellence, pouring his intensity into the sport to which he had turned because he was too intense for golf.

"Anything You Can Do, I Can Do Better"

He was a Renaissance overachiever. One day on *Who Do You Trust?* an expert archer gave a demonstration, after which Johnny proudly shot the arrows just as well. He blended his passion for perfection with great athleticism, so he tried to top every guest expert on both shows: the karate expert, who showed him how to break a board with his head; the woman holding the hula hoop record, which Johnny tried to break with his slim lithe body; and the contortionist who tried to twist Johnny into a pretzel. He wanted to be the kind of pretzel that would make a Budweiser ad.

In fact, his passion to be the best caused an embarrassing moment on *Who Do You Trust?* An expert fisherman demonstrated fly casting and then Johnny topped the fisherman by fly casting with more accuracy. For Johnny, it was always that line from *Annie Get Your Gun*—"Anything you can do, I can do better." I'm glad that the show never had a guest heart surgeon.

I remember Johnny spending an entire weekend in a hotel room to practice tricks for the show. More than just a magician, Johnny was also a ventriloquist who knew how to throw his voice. I knew how to throw mine, but it was always the same voice. He also taught himself how to play the guitar. He learned ballroom dancing and won an Arthur Murray jitterbug contest. In fact, Johnny was so competitive that when we went to state fairs, I had to act as his bodyguard in case he issued a challenge to the local middleweight champ.

Yes, life for Johnny was an endless salute to Vince Lombardi.

sixteen

Head of the Class

In the eulogies for Johnny after his death, many performers spoke of his rare class. None of them ever saw it as closely as I did.

One day when we were taping, he said to me during a commercial break, "Can I see you after the show?"

Well, I thought, *this is it. He's firing me, and I'll have to start a new career. I wonder how the opportunities are in refrigeration repair?*

On my way to his dressing room, I tried to figure out what I had done wrong. We always had worked so well together. Had he found someone with a louder laugh? Or someone who could hold "Heeeeere's Johnny!" even longer?

When I entered the dressing room, Johnny lit a cigarette, inhaled deeply, and said, "Ed, I just want you to know that I know what you're doing out there."

Screwing up, right? Oh well, The Tonight Show *would be a good credit on my résumé.*

Instead of dropping the ax, however, he said, "You're making me look good. You're out there just to make me look good."

A compliment from Johnny was rare. He presumed that everyone would do his job the way that Johnny did his—like a pro. Because my own nature is hearty, people don't suspect that compliments have always made me as uneasy as they made Johnny.

"Johnny, I've got to go," I said, hoping that my eyes wouldn't grow moist. "I've got a dinner date."

"Well," he said, "I just want to tell you that I know exactly what you're doing out there. You're out there only to make me look good."

No one, of course, had to make Johnny look good; he did that job splendidly alone. As I tried to flee from his moving words, he shouted, "You *see,* you can't take a compliment any more than I can!"

Johnny, of course, was right: my role was to make him look good while not looking too good myself. My job as straight man, as sidekick, as second banana, was to get Johnny to the punch line while seeming to do nothing at all. Through the years, many people felt that on *The Tonight Show,* I did nothing at all. Their dismissal of my work was the highest flattery.

I've always liked the story about the straight man who was walking on a beach when he suddenly heard a woman screaming, "Help! Help! I'm drowning!"

"You mean to say you're *drowning?*" he asked

Gentle Humor

What a thoroughly decent man Johnny Carson was. In thirty years of monologues, Johnny was careful never to hurt any person of whom he was making gentle fun.

I remember one show on which one of the guests was a woman whose talent, to use the word as loosely as it can be used, was to play coins by hitting them against a table to make sounds. When this woman came out, I was struck at once by how fat she was. She wore a pink dress that she not only filled but inflated. Some comics would have made an easy joke about her weight. Johnny, however, said with genuine warmth, "What a pretty dress."

Bad taste makes a lot of money in America, but Johnny showed another way to go. He showed that it was possible for a man to be tender as well as funny.

After the show, I told him, "You were sweet with that woman who looked like a pink weather balloon."

"A weather balloon?" he said. "She was the Hindenburg, but I wasn't going to blow her up. When you're three hundred pounds and come out in a pink dress to play coins, you're not just asking for humiliation, you're begging for it. Well, she wasn't going to get any help from me."

"Absolutely," I said. "Too easy to mock a poor thing like that."

"And cruel," said Johnny.

"We do get an occasional circus act, don't we?"

"The good ones are fine. But Ed, I'll never understand why so many people are dying to humiliate themselves on TV."

"Andy Warhol said everyone in America will be famous for fifteen minutes," I said.

"They should be fifteen that don't make you squirm."

Through the years, Johnny felt that, like so many celebrities, he had made his own children squirm, and I might have done the same to mine. My daughter Claudia was once watching a dramatic space launch with friends; and then they suddenly saw something less celestial—Claudia's father pitching beer.

Johnny, whose fame approached that of the president's, was always aware of the effect of that fame on his kids. On the last show, he said to them, "I hope that through the years your old man hasn't caused you too much discomfort."

The kind of class Johnny had is a vanishing quality in American performers, who seem to enjoy flaunting obscenity, underwear, and small arms. Johnny himself talked about it on a show that was a sentimental journey to his hometown of Norfolk, Nebraska.

"I come from the Midwest," he said, "and Midwestern values have always been important to me—openness, honesty, and a sense of warmth."

I never did a film with Cary Grant, probably because he didn't want the competition, but I did get to know Cary and had a few dinners with him. At every one, I asked him to come on *The Tonight Show*, but he always brushed off the request. Finally, at one of our dinners, I said, "Cary, you've just *got* to come on the show."

"Ed, I simply can't," he replied.

"But why?"

"Because it would break the illusion."

How much wiser was Cary Grant than today's film stars, who share with the public glossies of their colonoscopies. Of course, you can't break an illusion unless one is there to break. Johnny had the same wisdom about how his appeal was sustained by a certain separation from his fans.

"I do the show and then I go home," he once told me, "but I don't take it home with me."

Like every viewer in America, I knew that Johnny wasn't making hollow show business talk when he said on his last show, "It has been an honor and a privilege to come into your homes all these years to entertain you."

And all of us felt his deep sincerity when, during his final applause and the strains of "I'll Be Seeing You," he mouthed "I love you" and threw a kiss. That kiss on the air was the first time a Hollywood air kiss had any meaning.

From the Author's Collection

Before Johnny had his moment of truth in Fort Lauderdale and realized that golf was a gift from Satan, he and I tried to get a few tips from the great quarterback Sonny Jurgensen in Philadelphia.

Because Johnny had such high standards, he was upset the night that Tuesday Weld began behaving with a bit of arrogance. Johnny finally asked, "So tell me, what plans do you have for the future?"

And Tuesday replied, "I'll let you know when I'm back on the show next year."

"I haven't scheduled you again quite that soon," Johnny politely said, dispatching her with the lethal grace of Cyrano.

Of the twenty-two thousand guests who passed through *The Tonight Show,* Johnny fed all of them straight lines, appreciative laughter, and wit of his own. And once in a while, he graciously helped them get off.

I remember well a night when Peter O'Toole had come to us after forty-eight sleepless hours of filming and flying. The moment that Peter sat down, Johnny's radar detected what he called "the dancing eye syndrome." Seconds later, when O'Toole could not meet the challenge of speaking a complete English sentence, Johnny knew the man was in trouble and gently ushered him off the stage during the first commercial.

"I recognized the old syndrome at once," Johnny told me after the show. "Peter's eyeballs were twitching."

"There were nights when you and I could have been ushered off too," I said with a nostalgic smile.

"True," said Johnny, "but thirty million people weren't watching us at Sneaky Pete's."

seventeen

You Gotta Have Heart

One night in the fall of 1973, Johnny said, "I hear that whenever someone in the White House tells a lie, Nixon gets a royalty."

A few nights later, he said, "Did you know that Richard Nixon is the only president whose formal portrait was painted by a police sketch artist? By the way, Nixon isn't worried about the gas shortage and that's understandable, of course. Everything's downhill for him."

Not long after saying that line, Johnny realized that everything *was* downhill for Nixon and at a dismaying speed. He was crashing, and the compassion in Johnny kicked in.

"I've got to let up on Nixon now," he told me before one show. "He's going down the tubes fast, and I feel sorry for him."

And so, Johnny became the first person in show business to *stop* doing anti-Nixon jokes.

True Confessions

And now a confession: I once did some pro-Nixon work myself. In 1968, one of my neighbors was Robert Abplanalp, inventor of the aerosol can, who was one of Richard Nixon's best friends. At that time, one of my own best friends had an advertising agency that handled Abplanalp, and the two men helped Nixon make his comeback from oblivion. Aware of Nixon's poor appearance on television when debating John Kennedy, they asked me to coach him to look better.

As a favor to Nixon, I went to his office on New York's Park Avenue and taught him how to handle himself on *The Tonight Show*—how to smile, how to move his hands, how not to look like a member of a crime family.

When he finally did the show, he was relaxed and even charming, if a charming Richard Nixon doesn't strike you as an oxymoron.

"In the debates with Kennedy," Johnny said to Nixon, "you had that problem with five o'clock shadow. What are you going to do about it this time?"

"I'm going to steal your makeup man," Nixon said.

It was hardly a hilarious line, but for Richard Nixon the height of wit. He won that election without stealing any makeup, although at the Watergate . . .

The Manure Man

A few weeks after Nixon came to the show, Johnny's guest was a man from rural South Carolina named Frank Hill, who bore the proud title of the Manure Man. He did not, however, do anything as pedestrian as turn manure into fertilizer. No, Frank Hill came to *The Tonight Show* as the world's outstanding collector of artifacts made from quail droppings. He was also the world's *only* collector

NBC/Globe Photos, Inc.

The four stars who lit up late night for forty years: Steve Allen, Johnny, Jerry Lester, and Jack Paar.

of artifacts made from quail droppings. The quail-dropping field was pretty much all his.

Frank Hill came out to Johnny in a checkered shirt that hung outside his jeans, a baseball cap that sat on the back of his head, and muddy high shoes. He was, in short, what a fashion magazine would have called trailer-park trash. It would have taken no effort for Johnny to mock this country gentleman whose hobby was as ridiculous as a hobby could be—a bird-watcher of the wrong end.

Johnny, however, took a higher road and talked to Hill as if a fowl's feces were sculptor's clay. Although Johnny couldn't resist saying, "You're kind of the Cartier of Caca," he turned away from the toilet jokes so popular in American films today, and he didn't hold up Hill to cheap ridicule. Instead, Johnny showed genuine interest in how a feathered colon could produce art.

After twenty years on *The Tonight Show*, we had a celebration dinner. Johnny said to me, "Just keep pretending we know what we're doing, Ed."

Nate Cutler/Globe Photos

Nate Cutler/Globe Photos

When we were celebrating twenty years of *The Tonight Show,* Johnny and I were given a frame holding publicity pictures from both *Who Do You Trust?* and the early *Tonight Show.*

Delighted by the gracious treatment he had received, Hill ended his ten minutes of fame by presenting a gift that Johnny never would have found on Rodeo Drive—a large quail dropping paper holder for his desk.

"A big dropping for a big star," he said.

"I don't think I've ever been so moved, if you'll pardon the expression," said Johnny, blending humor with the decency deserved by a man who lived as far from Johnny's world as Venus.

Johnny showed the same compassion to Pee-wee Herman that he showed to the pink dirigible, Richard Nixon, and the Manure Man. After Pee-wee had been caught in warm self-involvement in a movie theater, Johnny might have been the only comedian not doing Pee-wee Herman jokes, in spite of great pressure from his writers.

"It's not that the joke is too easy, which of course it is," Johnny told me, "but I feel sorry for the poor guy. He did what every man in America has done, just not in a mezzanine."

On another show in the seventies, Johnny told some jokes about Wilbur Mills, the congressman who inexplicably had gone wading in Washington's Tidal Basin with a stripper named Fannie Fox. Good material for Johnny until the inexplicable became explicable to him.

"I found out he was an alcoholic," Johnny told me, "and so I had to stop. Alcoholism should never be spoofed."

eighteen

And Here's to Lewis and Clark!

Johnny wasn't an alcoholic and neither was I, but we didn't drink Ovaltine either. Through the years, he and I often went out for a few drinks after our shows. Ironically, my few were fewer than Johnny's few, even though I was the big Irishman and he was the slim WASP.

The morning after, our running joke was for Johnny to say, "Boy, Ed, were you wasted last night."

Of course, last night I had been, as always, not just the second banana but second with the grape.

One night, Johnny told America, "Actually, Ed has good control of his drinking. He drinks only in places that have walls."

Another night, he said, "Ed is very selective about his drinking. He drinks only to celebrate special occasions like Chinese New Year, Brazilian New Year, Bulgarian New Year, Arbor Day, and National Recycling Day."

And on still another night, he said, "Ed and I were out last night and I asked him why he drank so much. He said he drank to forget. I asked him, 'To forget what?' And he said he couldn't remember."

I allowed Johnny to create this besotted character for me because it played for laughs. And some of the laughs were my internal ones at thinking what the audiences never knew: that I was holding my liquor while Johnny's grip was not as tight. Moreover, this besotted character moved Anheuser-Busch to make me the spokesman for Budweiser, a product I had been testing for many years.

Johnny and I first began drinking together during the run of *Who Do You Trust?* On many days, the moment the show ended, I was ready to dash to Penn Station for a train back to my family in

From the Author's Collection

"And here's to Arbor Day!"

Philadelphia. And then Johnny asked, "Ed, you want to go get something to eat and drink?"

"Sure, Johnny, I'd love to," I always replied.

My going out with Johnny was more than just not wanting to say no to the boss. I also knew that this was a very nice guy whose company was a delight. And there was still one more reason. Although few people knew it, I was aware that Johnny's first marriage was breaking up. He just didn't have the energy for his home that he had for his studio, and he admitted it.

"If I had put the work into my marriages that I put into the show, they might have succeeded," he sadly said after his third divorce.

Here's to Arbor Day

I had arranged the first date with his third wife. He first saw this beautiful woman in the elegant restaurant 21 and asked me who she was.

"Her name is Joanna Holland," I said.

Holland was appealing country to him, so he made a date with her for what I realized would be October 23, his birthday. I arranged for Johnny and Joanna to have their first date at a fine old Spanish restaurant, where I had a musician play "Happy Birthday" on a flamenco guitar. On a flamenco guitar, "Happy Birthday" sounds like something that belongs not on Sesame Street but in Carnegie Hall.

Joanna was enchanted, but Johnny kept giving me looks that seemed to say, *The pain in Spain is when they entertain!*

We got through the rest of the dinner with no more serenading; and then, the three of us went to an after-hours place. When we were still there at its closing, I knew that a new Mrs. Carson might have appeared. Their feeling for each other was clearly strong, in spite of my company. It didn't last, however.

Johnny's feeling for a woman was to soar even higher several years later in Malibu, when he met Alexis, who in 1987 became his last and most beloved sweetheart.

Going out with Johnny after the shows put a strain on my own first marriage because my wife wanted me to continue being Mr. Philadelphia Television instead of Mr. New York Shot Glass with a buddy named Johnny.

And so, after the show, Johnny and I went somewhere and somewhere wasn't the Metropolitan Museum of Art. It was to places with other kinds of pictures, places called Sardi's, Jilly's, P. J. Clarke's, Michael's Pub, and Danny's Hideaway. And at those restaurants, Johnny unwound with three or four vodka sours, which was a mistake, not because they were poorly made—I can certify their quality—but because vodka is alcohol with no taste. It makes you high without telling you, and then, later in the evening, you wonder why you are suddenly falling on your face.

We usually began our undetectable infusions at Sardi's and then moved on to Danny's or Michael's or Jilly's, alternately laughing and being serious about the pressures on Johnny that the world never knew. Jack Paar had used his show as a confessional, but Johnny confessed only to me after taking some Smirnoff's truth serum. My bonding with him on those late afternoons and evenings was what he needed, but it still made me uneasy because both of us should have confined our use of alcohol to rubdowns.

From the Author's Collection

Toots Shor, king of a legendary New York restaurant, embracing Johnny and writer Jimmy Breslin. The man at the right may be a waiter.

Gradually, we were smart enough to decrease it. Drinking can make you either merry or surly; and Johnny knew that much of the time, he was in column B.

He once said of himself, "Three drinks of anything and I'm off to the races." I wouldn't have minded his going to the races, but sometimes he seemed headed for the ring.

"I've always been afraid I'd take a punch at someone," he told me.

"Even if you had to reach up," I said.

"Right; that's just it. It would be someone bigger and probably not a social worker, and then you'd have to do the show alone."

I was much bigger than Johnny, but I never wanted to have to

nineteen

Mr. Star Maker

Johnny launched the careers of more big stars than anyone in the history of show business, and I was at the launching pad to see them all take off.

I was there when a thin, nervous young woman said, "We lived in Westchester and my mother was worried that I wouldn't get married and would end up carrying a poodle to tables for one. In fact, she was so worried that she put a sign outside our house: "Last girl before thruway."

After delivering several other lines just as good, this young woman was invited to the couch and Johnny told Joan Rivers, "You're funny. You're going to be a star."

And I was there when a beefy older comic in a black suit kept patting his red tie and rocking back and forth while he said, "Oh, it was bad last week, Johnny, really bad. I bought a used car and my wife's dress was in the backseat. Oh, Johnny, it's always been bad. My wife met me at the door in a see-through negligee. She was coming home. Oh, bad, Johnny, bad. When I was born, I was so ugly that my mother slapped the doctor."

And then, shaking with laughter, Johnny invited Rodney Dangerfield to the couch, the cushioned rocket to stardom.

And I was there when a muscular young comedian said, "You know why my wife and I have five children? Because we didn't want

Courtesy of Stephen Cox collection

Johnny made an appearance on one of the early episodes of *Star Search*, which I hosted. I don't remember if he won.

six. Ah, the children. You know what my dream is? To have all the children out of the house before I die."

After which, Johnny certified that Bill Cosby would be a star.

He made the same certification when a short, skinny comic said, "I don't believe in the afterlife, but I'm still taking a change of underwear."

And Woody Allen was launched.

I always knew when Johnny was taking delight in a comedian's performance because he leaned on his left elbow with his wrist under his chin. When the comedian finished, that same hand waved him over to the couch and a career was sent into orbit. The comedian came to the couch to take my place and I moved down. That's how we knew when the show was over—when I reached the end of the couch. A smaller couch would have produced a half-hour show.

They weren't all comedians. Just four months into his New York run, Johnny made the first national presentation of a twenty-year-old singer who sang "Spring Can Really Hang You Up the Most" so ethereally that Johnny was visibly moved.

"When you sang," he told her, "the entire crew was utterly quiet. Usually, they're taking bets. You're an exciting new singer."

"Thank you," said Barbra Streisand, whose future even exceeded Johnny's praise.

Robert Goulet was an exciting new singer. Bobby Darin was an exciting new singer. But Barbra Streisand was a voice from paradise.

In addition to Rivers, Dangerfield, Cosby, Allen, and Streisand, many other stars owe either the launching or the speeding up of their careers to Johnny. Ironically, two of them were David Letterman and Jay Leno. And there were also Ray Romano, David Brenner, Ellen DeGeneres, Jerry Seinfeld, Drew Carey, Billy Crystal, Robin Williams, Phyllis Diller, Eddie Murphy, Bob Newhart, Don Rickles, Dick Cavett, Tim Allen, Garry Shandling, and Chris Rock.

I admired Johnny for having no jealousy of such comics, an attitude as rare as a bar mitzvah on the West Bank.

"I'm always glad when a young comedian gets our Friday night audience," he once said on the show. "It's good for him."

I loved the way Johnny lit up the night that George Carlin was a sportscaster who said, "Here's a partial score: Notre Dame, six."

And the night that Rodney Dangerfield said, "My mother didn't breast-feed me. She wanted me as a friend."

And the night that Bill Cosby said, "So I told my son who was misbehaving, 'Son, I brought you into this world, and I can take you out.'"

And the night that Chris Rock said, "Any time you find yourself on Martin Luther King Boulevard, get off."

And Johnny would have lit up for Elvis Presley because he was an Elvis fan, but Elvis's manager, a truly strange man named Colonel Parker, was afraid his star wouldn't have been able to carry on a spontaneous conversation in English on the air.

"Elvis don't got no interview skills," said Parker, who didn't speak much English himself.

Johnny had such wondrous skill at interviewing anyone from a tenor to a toddler that he would have made Elvis sound like Charlie Rose, or Pete Rose at least. Some of those he made stars came from meetings off the set.

Suzanne Somers

After doing a bit part in *American Graffiti,* Suzanne Somers auditioned for an NBC show called *Lotsa Luck* and was told to return in a couple of hours. Not knowing where to go, she decided to kill those two hours in the NBC commissary. Suddenly, in walked Johnny Carson and her heart started pounding. He was the greatest star, and she was the anonymous blonde at the wheel of a white Thunderbird in *American Graffiti.*

"Hi, little lady," said Johnny with a greeting more fitting for Aunt Blabby than a potential centerfold. "What are you doing here?"

"I'm waiting for a call back for a new show called *Lotsa Luck,*" said Suzanne. "And I've written a book of poetry."

Johnny had never heard such a non sequitur. He also had never seen a poet with the kind of couplet that Suzanne Somers carried on her chest.

"Well, I wish you lots of luck," said Johnny. "I hope you get the part."

M. Brennan-IPOL-Globe Photos, Inc.

Suzanne Somers, a poet Johnny discovered promoting her work beside the cream cheese in the NBC cafeteria, something Robert Frost forgot to do.

The next morning, Suzanne sent her book of poetry to Johnny, who at once invited her to be on the show. A few days later, standing behind the curtain, she heard Johnny introduce her and she wondered if she would be the first *Tonight Show* guest to ever throw up. Johnny, however, instantly put her at ease with his usual graciousness. And then she read some poems from the Jimmy Stewart School of Verse. She wasn't Emily Dickinson—or Angie either—and for some reason Johnny and I began to laugh. It was sophomoric, but Johnny and I spent a lot of time in the sophomore class, where our appreciation of poetry didn't go much beyond, "There once was a girl from Nantucket . . ."

"I didn't mind your laughing," Suzanne later told me. "I just didn't understand it."

"Suzanne," I said, "I never understand a lot of the show, but I apologize for two grown men acting like that."

"No problem. You know, Johnny made me funnier when we talked because he really listened."

"Yes," I said. "No one ever listens like Johnny."

"And I loved your chemistry with him, as if you had some secret joke going."

"Believe me, it was often a secret from us."

"Your interaction was so delicious."

"Yes, all the professional polish of a couple of kids kicking a can down the street."

After Johnny's quadruple heart bypass in 1999, Suzanne wrote him a long letter, pouring out her heart about what he had done for her career and how grateful she was and what he meant to all the people he had helped. A few days later she received this reply:

Dear Suzanne:

I'm fine. Really.

Johnny

twenty

A Detector Built In

Both on and off the air, two things made Johnny angry: rudeness and lack of professionalism.

Ray Charles was hardly unprofessional. However, while singing one night on the show, he suddenly called out to the drummer in Doc's band, "Pick up the pace!" The moment the show ended, Johnny went to Ray Charles's dressing room and said, "Ray, there's a drummer in Doc's band who needs an apology."

And that drummer got one—after a suggestion from a man who always knew the right way to behave. In fact, Ray apologized to the entire band.

Johnny was never able to suffer incompetents, frauds, or people who were simply ungracious. I have just described half the people in show business, but Johnny managed to avoid most of them because he had keen radar for bad behavior. Hemingway said that the best thing a writer can have is "a built-in shit detector." Hemingway would have admired Johnny's.

"My bugging point is low," he once said.

Johnny's standards were so high that Doc Severinsen told me he began to sweat every time Johnny came through the curtain because Doc was afraid he might screw up and have to face the wrath of a perfectionist who often sat alone for hours polishing his monologue.

Johnny had discovered Joan Rivers and created her stardom. He felt a special kinship for Joan, who went on to be his guest host ninety-three times, more often than Bob Newhart, David Brenner, David Letterman, or Jerry Lewis. When she became pregnant, he announced it on the show and later he announced the birth of her daughter, Melissa. And when Melissa was just a few days old, Joan had her delivered as a gift to Johnny with a note that said, "I weigh four pounds, three ounces. I eat very little. Please bring me up Jewish." Johnny held the sleeping baby in his arms for two hours, afraid to wake her.

"How's that for a sweet guy?" said Joan. "You know, if it hadn't been for Johnny, I'd still be playing lounges in Queens."

The sweet guy stopped talking to Joan, however, after she forgot to tell him first about an offer from Fox to have her own show.

It was a mistake I never made. I always went to Johnny to clear every offer I got for outside work. And *The Tonight Show* led to plenty of it for me, not just as the spokesman for Budweiser, Alpo, and the American Family Publishers, but also to a game show, a new talent show called *Star Search*, a show called *TV's Bloopers and Practical Jokes*, and as a substitute for Alan King in a Broadway play called *The Impossible Years*.

And as if all that weren't glitter enough, *The Tonight Show* also led to feature films for me. One was a remake of *An Affair to Remember,* in which Warren Beatty and Annette Bening also appeared, though they might feel it wasn't in that order. My favorite was a film with Jane Fonda called *Fun with Dick and Jane,* in which I played a heartily venal boss who fired George Segal. It was a great success for me. Columbia Pictures even took out newspaper ads to campaign for my getting an Oscar for best supporting actor. One reviewer said, "I knew Ed McMahon was in this movie because I saw the credits. But the moment I saw him on the screen, I forgot all about Johnny Carson."

However, *I* did not forget about Johnny Carson because all Johnny did was give me my life. No Oscar or Nobel Prize could have lured me away from *Fun with Johnny and Doc.*

My affection for Johnny was no illusion and no film career or other television show could ever have lured me away from him. In 1961, when Johnny was doing *Who Do You Trust?* he was tempted to leave when Carl Reiner asked him to be the star of a new sitcom about a suburban comedy writer named Rob Petrie. When Johnny turned down the offer, the role went to a young dancer named Dick Van Dyke.

It makes you wonder about life's turning points to think that coming home to Mary Tyler Moore and then falling over a hassock might have been the only man in show business who fell with as much comic flair as Dick Van Dyke.

Some of my outside work became a farm system for *The Tonight Show.*

There is a long tradition in American broadcasting of shows that discover new talent. A man named Major Bowes ran a talent

Courtesy of Stephen Cox Collection

Johnny studying the exquisitely timed stare of his idol, Jack Benny.

scout show on the radio called *The Amateur Hour*, and one night he discovered a quartet called the Hoboken Four, whose tenor was a skinny kid named Frank Sinatra. And on television, Arthur Godfrey did a show called *Arthur Godfrey's Talent Scouts* and discovered many future stars, although one of the losers was a young man with a guitar named Elvis Presley.

On *Star Search*, which ran for twelve years, I found people like Drew Carey, Rosie O'Donnell, Sinbad, Martin Lawrence, LeAnn Rimes, Dennis Miller, Beyoncé, and Usher. However, *Star Search* rejected Tim Allen and also Rodney Dangerfield. But maybe Rodney's rejection helped him to learn what no respect was. I've always wondered how we could have rejected a man who said such things as, "If it weren't for pickpockets, I'd have no sex life at all."

Fun with Dick and Jane

When I briefly became a movie star, Johnny couldn't resist the chance to interview me.

"*The Tonight Show* is indeed honored tonight," he said, "to have the first, and maybe the last, interview with America's newest film star. Please welcome him now . . . Ed McCann."

And out I came, saying, "It's Mc*Mahon.*"

"Clark Gable it's not," said Johnny. "Or Lassie. Ed, you used to be in television, I understand."

"I don't think you understand much. But yes, I used to do a daytime program called *Who Do You Trust?*"

"And what have you been doing since then?"

"Nothing. Absolutely nothing."

"And now you're in a new film called *Fun with Dick and Jane* with Jane Fonda and George Segal."

"I like to think they're in it with *me,*" I said.

"And there are men who like to think they are General Patton."

Continuing to keep a straight face, Johnny said, "In this film, you play a spacey boss?"

"No, a boss in the space industry. Although I know a spacey boss."

"Well, I hear you're quite good in *Fun with Dick and Jane.* Perhaps it will lead to other films for you."

For another five minutes, Johnny interviewed me in a tight two-shot, and then he said, "We've been joking here, of course—at least I *think* we have—but seriously, I want all our viewers to know that Ed is really good in this film. And I'm playing that as straight as I can play anything. Ed, you have my most heartfelt wish for a great film career."

"Thanks, Johnny," I said. "You know what that means to me."

"I hope so," he said. And then, when he stood up to shake my hand, the camera revealed that the bottom half of him was boxer shorts covered with hearts. He looked like an unmentionable valentine. I like to think that those hearts were for me, but they may have been for Dolly Parton.

twenty-one

His Own Multitude

The many characters Johnny played in his sketches were legendary—Carnac the Magnificent, Art Fern, Floyd R. Turbo, Aunt Blabby, Ronald Reagan, Rambo, Tarzan, El Moldo, the Easter Bunny, Shirley Temple, and Count Dracula. And he did it with an uncanny instinct for what was funny. The script was always just a runway from which he took off, often in surprising directions. The most challenging part of my job was following him.

For example, during one monologue early in 1977, Johnny found that certain words were coming from his mouth as if he were speaking Ukrainian.

"*Yetserday,* U.S. Steel announced . . . ," he said, and then he wrinkled his brow in mock alarm, paused, and asked me, "Ed, do you find that *yesterday* is a particularly hard word to pronounce?"

"No, Johnny," I replied. "I say it successfully all the time. Once even yesterday—not to make you feel bad about it."

Johnny was feeling anything but bad. He was preparing for take-off. "Yesterday," he sang, "all my troubles seemed so far away. Now it looks as though they're here to stay. Oh, I believe in yesterday."

At this point, Doc's band had sneaked in an accompaniment and I began to hum, making sure that Johnny held the lead as our cockamamie chorusing continued. We were no threat to the Beatles or even to the Slugs. We were more like a couple of guys at whom people on the street toss coins.

Finally, perhaps because he feared that word of this performance might reach Paul McCartney, Johnny stopped and said, "Now what was I talking about? Oh, yes. *Yesterday*."

But refusing to let him off the hook, Doc Severinsen began the music again and Johnny plunged into a second chorus, after which he silenced the band with a karate chop. There was loud applause and then as long a pause.

Where can he go from here? I wondered.

Johnny knew where, saying, "About twelve hours ago, U.S. Steel announced . . ."

With the audience roaring, he said to me, "That's what makes this job what it is."

"Just what is it?" I asked.

With a frown of genuine puzzlement, Johnny said, "I don't know."

Johnny had turned a slip of the tongue into another inspired flight.

"Okay, that's over," he said. "Now what do we do for fun?"

"Let me get back to you on that," I replied.

"Two grown men," said Johnny.

"Graduates of major universities," I said.

This wacky climate that Johnny created turned unlikely people into comedians. In a tongue-twisting routine called the Copper Clapper Caper, Johnny became the first and last man to ever make Jack Webb funny. He did the same to John Wayne, who turned to me and said, "I'm not drinking anymore, Ed."

"Really?" I said.

"Does tequila count?"

That night, I went to dinner with John Wayne to further explore the proper scoring of tequila.

Art Fern—Host of *Tea Time Movie*

Johnny's character of Art Fern was host of *Tea Time Movie,* which presented matinees of such unforgettable films as *Gidget Takes on Fort Ord, Ma and Pa Kettle Host an Orgy, The Merry Widow Has a Change of Life, Abbott and Costello Visit a Leper Colony,* and *Debbie Flunks Her Wasserman.* Turner Classic Movies may have introductions to great films by distinguished directors like Sydney Pollack, but Sydney is a tongue-tied amateur compared to Art Fern's introductions of the cinematic swill on *Tea Time Movie.*

Of course, it was hard to look at Johnny because next to him was always Carol Wayne, whose breasts should have been designated as national landmarks. It may have been tea time, but all I could think of was milk. With Carol Wayne's bosom beside him, and partly ahead of him too, Johnny often gave *Tea Time Movie* an

R rating. In one pre-movie commercial for some sexual aid, Art Fern asked, "Has romance gone out of your relationship? Does your bed move only during an earthquake? Does your wife keep a can of mace on the night table? Are you tired of hearing, 'That's it?'"

Because I'm such a deeply sentimental guy—I cry at beer commercials (the ones I didn't do)—my favorite *Tea Time Movie* was *Andy Hardy Gets a Girl in Trouble,* starring Hoot Gibson, Henry Gibson, Dean Stockwell, Jimmy Dean, and Dean Rusk. Art Fern's introduction to it should be carved on the entrance to a landfill.

> Some of you folks who are repeating the sixth grade may have trouble understanding the plot of *Andy Hardy Gets a Girl in Trouble.* You see, Andy Hardy lived in an innocent time, when everyone was a little stupid and nobody knew how babies were made. That information was first released by Alfred Kinsey, but to naive little Andy, Kinsey was the friendly neighborhood bookie and Trojans were only at USC.

Aunt Blabby

Aunt Blabby was another Carson character, for which we never rehearsed because we never rehearsed for *anything.* We just went to his office, looked at the cards, and then winged it. However, if I had winged it when flying for the Marine Corps the way Johnny and I did one night with Aunt Blabby, I would have left myself on a Korean mountainside.

Johnny was supposed to be my comic copilot, but on that particular night he took his hands off the controls to see if I could fly solo. The happy opening gave no sign of the crash to come.

"I'm old and dense," Aunt Blabby said. "*One* would be enough."

"One *would* be enough," I said.

"Why do you repeat everything? I can get that at a Taco Bell."

And then came an ominous moment, when I asked, "I've been wondering, Aunt Blabby, what do you think of a May-December marriage?"

"Well, they have a hell of a Labor Day," she replied.

The studio was like a library.

"Oh, really?" I asked, knowing that Johnny would save it.

"Where does it say, 'Oh, really?'"

There was a smattering of laughter.

"You know, just for fun, maybe we could do some jokes instead."

There was a big laugh and I relaxed. That was a mistake.

"Aunt Blabby, I hear you just traveled overseas. Did you make it to Italy?"

There was silence from Johnny.

"To Italy," I said. "It's near Yugoslavia. Also Greece."

More silence from Johnny.

"Do you want to expand on that?" I asked, picturing viewers flipping to the Weather Channel. It was certainly getting hot onstage.

I was wondering if there might be any work for me at CBS when Johnny finally said, "No, I don't."

"Don't want to talk about that?"

"You got it."

"I hear there are a lot of statues in Italy," I said, getting a big laugh while wanting to put Aunt Blabby in a home.

"I didn't know that," Johnny said, and the explosion of laughter revealed that the two of us had finally come out of the tunnel before crashing into another train.

"Now that you've found your voice, Aunt Blabby, tell me this," I said. "You're a handsome woman . . ."

"And you're Ray Charles."

"Do you go out on many dates?"

"Not only can I not get a date," Aunt Blabby said, "but men come into my house to steal my calendars."

I am interviewing Aunt Blabby, who had managed not to age gracefully.

NBC/Globe Photos

twenty-two

The Man with ESPN

Sometimes when I feel blue, I think of the improvised exchanges I had with Johnny's character that we loved as much as we loved Aunt Blabby and Carnac. He was El Moldo, the mindless mentalist who had a remarkable consistency—he *never* knew what anyone was thinking, including himself. El Moldo was always blindfolded, but he would have been equally clueless with his eyes open.

For our El Moldo routine, I went into the studio audience the way Steve Allen had done.

"I have a lady, El Moldo," I called to Johnny, who now wore the slick black hair that he also used for Count Dracula.

"Good, get one for me," he replied.

"Can you tell me, O Omniscient El Moldo, what is on this woman's mind?" I asked.

"No," said Johnny, "and it's good she doesn't know what's on *my* mind, particularly if she can dial 911. Of course, maybe she still wants a medium and I'm a medium who's rare."

"There are those who think you are also done."

"And there are those who may hire *you* in another medium, now that you are about to leave this one."

"You make fun, El Moldo."

"This sounds like fun to you? Clearly not to all the other people in here."

"El Moldo, this woman has heard much about the state of your mind."

"So has the Menninger Clinic. They've offered me a scholarship."

"Before you accept it, allow this woman to be dazzled by your awesome power. She is thinking of a number between one and three."

"A number between one and three . . ."

"That's what I just said. I'm glad to see you have a good memory."

"I wish I could remember the name of my agent."

"El Moldo, can you tell this woman what her number is?"

"She is thinking of a number between one and three . . . between one and three . . . That means she is thinking of it after lunch."

"No, O Pseudo-insightful One, we are talking about the *number*, not the time of day."

"I don't get it. I don't get a lot."

"Well, can you tell her what time of day it is right *now*? Little children can do that."

"Then find one and leave me alone. I'm thinking of getting out of show business."

"I didn't know you were in it."

"May a crystal ball drop down your drawers."

"Before you're done, O Demi-Nostradamus . . ."

"Nostra who? Is that some new crime family?"

"Before you're done . . ."

"Medium, that's how I'm done."

Taking off my watch and holding it in the air, I asked, "Tell me, O Dean of Rare Divining, what am I holding in my hand?"

"It should be your résumé. But I've never seen one with a strap."

From the Author's Collection

Johnny set the tone of *The Tonight Show* by opening the very first program with a monologue. It was terrific and he went on to perfect the art in more than 4,000 monologues over the next thirty years.

The El Moldo routines inspired Johnny to walk the highest high wire, saved from falling again and again by his lightning wit.

"El Moldo," I said to him one night, "I have a gentleman here for you."

"I don't collect gentlemen," Johnny replied. "Does he have a sister? Or a very young mother?"

"How you jest, El Moldo."

"I'm glad it sounds like jesting to somebody."

"Would you care to guess where this gentleman lives?"

Courtesy of Stephen Cox Collection

Johnny, when *The Tonight Show* was broadcast from New York, was always selective in letting himself look ridiculous.

"He's forgotten?"

"No, he remembers, and he wonders if you can divine his particular city."

"All right . . . let me divine . . . What does that mean?"

"To see it."

"Ah, yes. I see . . . Seattle."

"I hate to say this, El Moldo, but you're wrong."

"And *you're* wrong if you think I'm going to stay in this sketch. When's the next bus to Seattle?"

"To get back to your divining, El Moldo—"

"Any reason why?"

"So you see Seattle—"

"I didn't say he lives there. I just said I see it. I see a garbage truck too."

"Would you care to name another city, El Moldo?"

"I don't think I know another . . . No, wait a moment . . . Yes, I see Kansas City."

"Wrong."

"Sioux City?"

"Wrong."

"Dodge City?"

"Wrong."

"He once drove a Dodge through a city."

"Would you rather predict something else, El Moldo?"

"Yes. One more sketch like this and you're on your way back to selling Johnny Mops in Philadelphia."

At other times, Johnny was the great astronomer, Carl Sagan.

"Good evening, Dr. Sagan," I would say.

"But not in China," Johnny might reply, "where it is morning and where your 'Hi–yooo!' might have great meaning in Cantonese."

"And what would that great meaning be?"

"It would be that if we continue to sustain the particular quality of material like this, we'll be replaced by Lawrence Welk, who's dead and sounding better than us."

"I will think about that, Doctor, but not too long. Tell me, do you happen to be any relation to the famous French writer, Françoise Sagan?"

"No. Do you happen to be any relation to Bigfoot?"

"Speaking of big, a young man on parole in Texas has asked me to ask you this question about the cosmos."

"You mean all that space or the soccer team?"

"All that space. Can you tell these students what followed the Big Bang?"

"I believe it was called the Big Cigarette."

twenty-three

The World's Coolest Star

In the nearly fifty years that I knew him, never once did I see Johnny play "the star." Devoid of visible ego, he was flawlessly gracious with everyone. On the air, he was even gracious in deflating the mighty. His wit was paradoxical because it was both gentle and lethal. Barbara Howar, the Washington columnist, once told me that the moment Johnny started making jokes about someone, that someone's career was over.

For example, when Johnny began calling Secretary of Agriculture Earl Butz "Earl the Pearl," Butz fell faster than grain in a silo. And when Johnny began doing casual jokes about the folly of the Vietnam War, Lyndon Johnson knew the war was lost. Johnny could always sense the mood of America very quickly.

The great exception, of course, was Ronald Reagan. Johnny

had to keep him around so he could say such things as: "There is a power struggle going on between President Reagan's advisors. Moe and Curly are out. Larry is still in."

And "President Reagan just signed a new law, but I think he was in Hollywood too long. He signed it, 'Best wishes, Ronald Reagan.'"

Johnny also loved playing Reagan in sketches.

"Mr. President," the interviewer would say.

"Yes, that's what it says on my checks," Johnny would reply, made up as Ronald Reagan. "My Social Security card also says number one, but I think that's for when it was issued. Want to trade it for a Shirley Temple? A Shirley Jones? A Tom Jones?"

"Mr. President, you've called the Soviet Union the Evil Empire—"

"That used to be MGM, but I think Louis B. Mayer may have died. I may have too. So hard to keep track."

"Well, let me ask you a different question."

"Yes, I've already forgotten that one."

"What do you plan to do about Red China?"

"Replace some of it with blue china," he said, "but only for dinner. Red china is perfectly fine for lunch. Say, how do you like the movies now that they're talkies?"

"Speaking of talking, Mr. President," the interviewer would say, "do you ever watch *The Tonight Show*?"

"Only when the Weather Channel is doing reruns. That guy who says 'Hi-yooo!' gets on my nerves. Can't they find some hogs for him to call?"

"Mr. President, what do you plan to do about the poor?"

"The poor what?"

"The poor material in this sketch."

"Impeach the writers."

No matter how poor the material might have been, Johnny was still most alive when that camera light was on. How did he relax and drain his intensity when the camera was off? With leisurely dinners and drinks after the show. In some of our New York spots, like Jilly's, Michael's Pub, and Danny's Hideaway, Johnny often finished the evening by playing the drums to a jazz beat, while I pretended I could sing. When the show moved to Los Angeles, we went to a restaurant on Sunset Boulevard called Sneaky Pete's, where he also played the drums with the band while I held forth with a singing voice that should have been limited to "Heeeeere's Johnny!" and "Hi-yooo!"

Johnny as Ronald Reagan, an actor who got the only gig better than *The Tonight Show*.

Globe Photos, Inc.

Properly Ridiculous

For years, Doc Severinsen and I tried to get Johnny to play his drums on the show.

"Ed, I just can't do it," he said. "I don't want to look ridiculous."

Johnny wanted to look ridiculous only when being ridiculous was part of his comic art: Carnac the Magnificent, El Moldo, Aunt Blabby, Ronald Reagan, Art Fern, the thirsty Count Dracula, the Marlon Brando of the Mighty Carson Art Players, and the dumb rube Floyd R. Turbo, who said, "If God didn't want man to hunt, he wouldn't have given him plaid shirts."

Looking properly ridiculous was not an oxymoron for Johnny.

"An oxymoron, Ed?" I can hear him saying. *"What's that? A moron who studies at Oxford?"*

Yes, properly and splendidly ridiculous. For example, men in drag have always been a drag to me, about as funny as *The Wit of Kim Il Sung*. It's sophomoric corn, even though some juniors and

Floyd R. Turbo, whose profound wisdom included, "The army prepares you for life. It teaches you how to crawl on your belly, which comes in handy when you're looking for a job."

Courtesy of Stephen Cox Collection

seniors do it too. The night that Johnny dressed as a floozie in a low-cut white dress and his wig fell off, he showed me the one man who could make drag funny.

Johnny being funny in drag was like jazz: you couldn't analyze or explain it. You either got it or you didn't. When Johnny's wig fell off, he said, "This is your life, Phyllis Diller!" but he didn't have to say a thing; his comic moves were like those of a great dancer or tennis player. Instinctively, he was doing it right and it was lovely to see.

One facet of Johnny's class was his always wanting to make guest comedians look good instead of wanting to compete with them. With never a trace of jealousy, he was happy to play a straight man to all of them. I can still see him breaking up when George Gobel said to him, "Did you ever think that the whole world was a tuxedo and you were a pair of brown shoes?"

Was that the funniest line ever said on the show that didn't come from Johnny? Perhaps. There were so many. The one from Johnny that has kept me smiling through the years was this Carnac moment:

"And here is the answer, O Magnificent One," I said.

"The answer may be to replace this with decent material," Johnny said, holding the envelope to his forehead. "Sis, boom, bah."

"Sis, boom, bah," I said as Johnny shot me a look that said, *May a mouse relieve himself in your martini.*

And then he opened the envelope to read, "What is the sound of a sheep exploding?"

I also smile when I think of Carnac's answer "Ben Gay."

Johnny put the envelope to his head and then read, "Why didn't Franklin have any children?"

And I will never stop smiling at the memory of Johnny's exchange one night with Mr. Universe.

"Remember," Mr. Universe told him, "your body is the only home you will ever have."

"Yeah," said Johnny, "my home is pretty messy, but I have a woman come in once a week."

With his flawless taste, the naughty innocent from Nebraska knew exactly how far he could go.

twenty-four

No Ice in Those Veins

I wish that America could have heard some of the off-camera talk between Johnny and me.

Every year, we called each other on our birthdays. His was October 23; mine is March 6. His gift to me, even in the last year of his life, was always the same—a new joke.

"Happy birthday, Ed," he said one year.

"Thanks, Johnny," I said. "Is the Rolls on its way over?"

"I thought about a Rolls," he said, "but would you want to break our tradition?"

"I would."

"I didn't think so. And here's your joke. Do you know what the captain of the *Titanic* said?"

"No, Johnny, what did the captain of the *Titanic* say?" I replied.

"That's just the tip of the iceberg."

On another March 6th, he said, "Happy birthday, Ed. And here's your joke":

> A couple with a six-year-old daughter named Agnes is building a new house across the street from their old one and they want her to see how a house is built. And so, every day little Agnes goes across the street and watches the construction. When the house is finished, the head of the construction crew says, "Agnes, you really helped us build this house and we appreciate that, so here are three gifts for you: a hard hat, a hammer, and a dollar."
>
> When Agnes brings her gifts home, her mother says, "Oh, those are lovely gifts, Agnes. We'll have to put that money in the bank so you can watch it grow the way you watched the house grow."
>
> The next day, Agnes and her mother take the dollar to the bank, where the manager accepts it and says, "Agnes, this is wonderful. The first dollar you ever made. Tell me, are you going to build *more* houses?"
>
> "No," she says.
>
> "No?" asks the manager. "Why not?"
>
> "Do you have any idea how long it took the morons to deliver the Sheetrock?"

Morons is my softer word for you and your family; in telling the joke to me, Johnny had used a less elegant one. He had heard that inelegant word many times in the Navy, where he had been an ensign, just as I had heard it many times in the Marines, where I had been a colonel. And that difference in our military ranks fed a lighthearted rivalry between us.

"I used to be in charge of groups of sailors who'd come back from the Pacific at the end of the war," he told me, "and I had a lot of trouble saying 'Men' so it didn't sound as though it was coming from Loretta Young."

"Yes," I said, "those men weren't used to soprano commands. Did any of them ever obey you? Did any of them ever *hear* you?"

"Of course," said Johnny, "with that boom of yours, Colonel, you could have called in the whole Third Fleet."

"It might've helped if you had told them you had ice water in your veins," I said. "Well, it all turned out well. You finally found a use for that voice. And it's still getting laughs."

Andrea Renault-Globe Photos

In 1992 when Johnny got an award for being such a great communicator, I thought that it was like honoring a lark for singing well.

One reason for the myth of ice water in Johnny's veins was that socially he *seemed* aloof. But he wasn't aloof; he was merely shy, and he told me the reason. "I guess I'm a loner," he said, "because I like having control. That's important to me. On the show, I'm in command. It's tough to do that at a party, unless it's the Nazi Party, of course."

"Yes," I said, "no cameras in living rooms."

"You know," he told me, "I'm better with cameras than people. I'd do better if people had little red lights in the middle of their foreheads."

But the people at cocktail parties had no red lights, just red lips and sometimes reddish noses, and Johnny never felt comfortable being with them.

"I wish I could be like you," he once told me. "You're so *hearty.* Mr. Sunshine; you're everyone's friend. It's really depressing."

Yes, Johnny Carson, who had America at his feet, envied his second banana when the cameras were off. At parties, it wasn't "Heeeeere's Johnny!" but "Where's Johnny?"

His least entertaining trick was making himself disappear. He was usually in a corner doing magic, making cigarettes vanish, or rolling coins or flipping cards. He was happiest doing card tricks, especially if they were for children. Johnny connected wonderfully with people of all ages. Both on and off the show, he was just as good with a three-year-old who liked magic as he was with a waiter of 105 who could run with a tray that held two beers and two glasses—a sudsy centenarian who belonged in a new Olympic event.

I was supremely lucky to be one of the people who did have a red light in his forehead for Johnny because he often performed privately for me. I do not say this boastfully because other close

Courtesy of Stephen Cox Collection

At Johnny's sixtieth birthday party, he really did make me this happy. I'm not that good an actor.

friends of his have told me that Johnny often performed for their audience of one.

One night when I was on Johnny's boat, he suddenly was moved to do the equivalent of twelve monologues: jokes, impressions, and stories just for me that lasted for an hour and a half. It was the greatest one-man nautical performance since Moses played that little joke on the Egyptians. And halfway through a dinner for six people at Frank Sinatra's house, Johnny stood up and did a fifteen minute monologue, as if he had just come through the curtains. For Johnny, those curtains hung in many more places than Burbank's Studio One.

One Friday early in the New York run of *The Tonight Show,* Johnny said, "Let's go down to Fort Lauderdale for the weekend.

We won't go crazy. Just have a healthful three days. We'll relax, have some fun, play golf."

"Johnny, I'm rotten at golf," I said.

"I'm worse than that," he said. "Hell, I gave it *up*, but we'll just go out on the course and soak up some sun."

"It might be more fun not to play golf."

The following day, we flew to Fort Lauderdale and checked into a hotel that had just been refurbished and was barely occupied, where we were given connecting suites on the second floor. When the bellman took up our luggage, he said with a wink in his voice, "Fellas, I'll leave open this door between the suites so the girls can walk back and forth."

He must have thought we were on a spring break from a school that had sophomores of forty.

"If any girls walk back and forth," I told him, "they'll be in the wrong suite."

Early the following morning, Johnny and I decided to enjoy the sunrise. Wearing only jockey shorts—but the finest brand, of course—we walked out to the balconies of what we presumed was an empty hotel. And it was empty, except for a couple just below us, who were being shown around the refurbished hotel by one of the staff.

Suddenly, the staff man spotted a celebrity fashion show. And calling the attention of the couple to a sight considerably rarer than the rising sun, he pointed to the jockey shorts of one of America's most debonair men and cried, "Look up, Mrs. Thompson!"

There are no picture postcards of that particular scene.

twenty-five

When the Jokes Were on Us

Without doubt, the party that Johnny disliked more than any other was not a real party, but a practical joke I pulled on him for my show, *Bloopers and Practical Jokes,* when Johnny and I were in London with Brandon Tartikoff, the head of NBC programming. Because Johnny liked Brandon, Brandon was able to lure him to a party supposedly filled with people worth meeting. These people, however, were actually minor English actors and worth meeting only if you found value in meeting minor English actors.

As he entered the cocktail party with me, Johnny asked, "Are these people really worth meeting? Or do they want to borrow money?"

"Johnny, they're potential sponsors of the Wimbledon telecast," I said, knowing the only thing they could sponsor would be a kid applying to Eton.

At the party, all the actors played as if auditioning for *Oliver Twist.* One by one, they talked to Johnny in accents so thick that Johnny was looking for an interpreter. Even spoken intelligibly, their words still would have been unintelligible.

"Old fellow," said one of them to Johnny, "tosh blowsis arfing ah riss rowse viding wot brudderr. Isn't that right, old chap?"

"You could put it that way," said Johnny to a man who was making Buddy Hackett sound like Laurence Olivier.

"Ah, Carson, blessum ah tumley dumster posh pratter. Eh?" said another.

"There are those who feel that way," said Johnny, wondering if he had fallen down the royal rabbit hole.

From the Author's Collection

Johnny and I on a rare golf outing at a Philadelphia country club before we both gave up the insane game that is "a good walk spoiled." Included in this group were Sonny Jurgensen (at my left) and Tom Brookshier (at Johnny's left), both of whom played for the Philadelphia Eagles at the time.

And then, after hearing more of Her Majesty's aliens, Johnny suddenly turned to me and said, "You'll pay for this. And you'll never know when."

"Meet just one more. His name is Sir Gordon. Two grown men," I said, shaking with laughter.

"No, only one," said Johnny. "And one rotten child who reminds you that you'll never know when."

He had already decided to remember Brandon Tartikoff and me for having arranged this little joke. He couldn't do anything to Brandon, but unfortunately I didn't run NBC. And so, for me there would be a "when."

"When" came a few weeks later in Burbank. After a taping, I left the NBC studio in a limousine driven by an old friend named Patrick. On the way to the gate, we passed a sign: "All cars are subject to inspection."

A good idea, I thought. *All cars should be inspected for impurities.*

At the gate, we stopped and a guard told Patrick to open the trunk.

"Nothing in there but Jimmy Hoffa," I called to him. He must have loved hearing car trunk gags.

When he opened the trunk, the guard didn't find Jimmy Hoffa, but he found something worse: a huge collection of NBC equipment—typewriters, calculators, staplers, even a phone. The only thing missing was a peacock.

Putting his head in the car, Patrick said, "Mr. McMahon, he wants you to step out."

"Oh, I can sign the autograph in here," I said.

"No, there's a lot of NBC property in the trunk, and I have no idea how it got there."

As I sat there stunned and bewildered, someone else in uniform approached the car. I was so flustered that I didn't recognize a guard named Johnny. He was wearing lieutenant's bars. NBC security had taken him in grade as a transfer from the Navy.

"Would you like to call a lawyer or one of your English sponsors?" he asked.

Exploding with laughter, I said, "I'd like to ask Carnac how he got all that stuff in there."

"By remembering the wonderful time Carnac had at a cockamamie cocktail party."

twenty-six

Just One of the Kids

The proof of the temperature of Johnny's heart was how much children liked him. You can fake warmth with adults, but you never can fake it with children. They have unerring phoniness detectors.

It was heartwarming to watch Johnny one night when his guests were two second-grade girls in fluffy white dresses and big hair bows. They were marketers of jokes.

"It's nice to meet you both," Johnny sweetly said. "Are you comfortable?"

Some of Johnny's guests would have said, "Comfortable? I make a living." But these two fetching children simply said, "Oh, yes."

"You're both very pretty," Johnny said. "Have you ever seen this show before?"

"Yes," said one, "but I fell asleep."

"Why should you be any different from all the adults? Now, I hear you sell jokes. How much do you charge for a joke?"

"A penny," said one of the girls.

"That's what most of mine are worth. Tell me one."

"Why does an anteater never catch colds?" asked one of the girls.

"Gee, I don't know," said Johnny. "Why does an anteater never catch colds?"

"Because it's full of little anti-bodies."

Giving the girls a penny, Johnny said, "I like that; I'll buy another."

"Did you hear that Willie Nelson got hit by a car?" asked one of them.

"No, I missed that news," said Johnny.

"He was playing on the road again."

"And what do you call a cow that just had a baby calf?" asked the other.

"A proud mother?" said Johnny.

"No, a decalfinated cow."

"Those are really good jokes," said Johnny, "and you tell them very well."

Never did Johnny's class shine more brightly than when he was talking to children as if they were adults.

Johnny's wit was so fast that he was rarely topped. However, topped he was, and unforgettably one night, by a child of eight named Joey Lawrence.

When Joey came out, Johnny was as warm as he always was to children. In a sweetly paternal voice, he asked, "Joey, have you ever seen this show before?"

"Yes," said Joey. "One night when I was throwing up."

While the explosive laughter was sustained, Johnny did the longest silent take I had ever seen, an exquisite blend of amusement, consternation, and resignation.

And then he said, "Between vomits, you looked in on us?"

"Yes," said Joey.

"Well, we like to get 'em early and have them grow up and throw up with us."

Johnny had done as well as he could. My own hero, W. C. Fields, could have warned him that you perform with children at your own risk.

On another night, Johnny lovingly interviewed—and *lovingly* is the proper word—a seven-year-old actress named Kaleena Kiff, who was appearing in a new NBC sitcom with Tony Randall, the kind for which Johnny also might have to read, "Coming Thursdays at 9:30 is *Love, Sidney,* in which Tony Randall hates his mother so much that he spites her by hating all women and seducing some men. And hilarity ensues."

When Kaleena said that her birthday was October 23, Johnny said, "October 23? No kidding! That's *my* birthday too! We're Virgo, but on the cusp of Libra. I'm proud to share a cusp with you."

Johnny looked at Kaleena as though he were about to adopt her. My man W. C. Fields would have said, "Get your own birthday, kid."

However, children brought out all the sweetness that was in Johnny.

"What do you think of Tony Randall?" he asked.

"He's one of the nicest people I've ever met," said Kaleena.

"And that's just what he said about *you* when he was on this show. Tell me, Kaleena, have you ever seen *The Tonight Show*?"

"Three times."

"Some kind of punishment, I guess. Do you have any brothers or sisters?"

"No, but my mom is about to have one."

"That's great. Do you want a brother or a sister?"

"A brother. My friends tell me a sister drives you bananas."

"You can make that drive with a brother too. I have one and he's made me pick lots of fruit. Well, Kaleena, it's been very nice to meet you."

"Yes," said Kaleena, agreeing that it was nice to meet her.

"And you come back," said Johnny with a look that could have been coming from the father of the bride.

twenty-seven

This Is Ed McMahon, Going Bananas

The memories of the wild wackiness of the show still burn brightly for me. One particularly crazy episode was the night of what I call the Great Egg Toss. It all began when Dom DeLuise came out to do an elaborate trick. He put five raw eggs on top of matchbooks that covered five glasses of water standing on a tray.

"I'm going to hit this tray with this broom handle," said Dom, "and all the eggs will fall into the glasses."

Johnny, of course, knew much more impressive tricks, but he was a good sport and pretended that Dom's trick required more skill than could be flaunted by a six-year-old.

"I'm going to count to three," said Dom.

"You can get that high, can you?" said Johnny. "That's trick enough."

"All right . . . one . . . two . . . three!"

Dom smacked the tray and all the eggs fell into the glasses. Always competitive, Johnny now had to jump in and show Dom how he could juggle three eggs. Perhaps a bit jealous of Johnny's legerdemain, Dom then tossed an egg at Johnny to see if Johnny knew how to take one on the head. Johnny returned the favor and threw a couple of eggs at Dom; and then Johnny thoughtfully included me in the fun by throwing an egg at me.

"Heeeeere's scrambled!" I cried and threw the egg back, while Johnny and Dom exchanged a few more. The three of us were making a sentimental return to nursery school. And now, with his magician's hands, Johnny cracked one egg over Dom's head while dropping another inside his pants.

"You're insane!" Dom cried. "You guys are *bananas*!"

Taking that as a slur on my good name, even though a banana I proudly was, I took another egg, cracked it, and dropped it down Dom's pants, feeling that he certainly would have wanted two eggs sunny-side up.

Moments later, the three of us were a late-night omelet.

"Did you like your eggs over easy?" Johnny asked me after the show.

"When I sit on them, I like a little salt," I replied.

"Two grown men."

"Graduates of major universities."

Anything for a Laugh

The following year, when one of these graduates had whipped cream squirted down his pants by Burt Reynolds, Johnny grabbed the can and I expected him to put a similar topping on Burt's undershorts. Instead, however, Johnny again proved himself a master of the unexpected by squirting more whipped cream into his own shorts and then smiling in contentment. Every other comedian would have squirted Reynolds; but Johnny again proved his originality by turning his own privates into the cupcake.

One of the things I loved most about Johnny was that he would do anything for a laugh. I've mentioned the night he allowed a tarantula to crawl up his arm. There is not enough money in Bill Gates's portfolio for me to do that. Another night, he broke a wooden panel with his head. And on still another, he fell from a high platform into an air bag—no, not an author promoting a book.

He once made a trampoline jump so high that he flew off camera. And one night, a special-effects man was explaining how a soldier in a foxhole was blown into the air by triggering a hidden explosion under a platform. Well, Johnny proceeded to die for NBC.

His build was slight, but his reservoir was deep.

A guest on one show began talking about the two cartoonists who invented Superman in the thirties.

"No," said Johnny, "Nietzsche invented Superman long before that, but he changed only in German phone booths. He flew with the Red Baron, I believe."

I had studied philosophy at Catholic University and I wondered if Johnny had studied philosophy too. After the show, I asked, "Johnny, *Nietzsche*? Where the hell did *that* come from?"

Tapping his head, he said, "Ed, I never throw anything away."

Johnny, in fact, had a mental file of German philosophers.

One night, he asked Fernando Lamas, "Why did you go into movies?"

"Because it was a great way to meet broads," Lamas said.

"Schopenhauer couldn't have put it better," Johnny replied.

I also try never to throw anything of value away, especially good wine; but one night on the show, I almost threw some on Johnny. It was another one of those spontaneous moments that lit up the show for thirty years.

In doing a commercial for a competitor of Saran Wrap, I was to take a goblet of red wine, cover it with this wrap, and then turn it upside down to dramatically demonstrate that the wrap wouldn't leak. However, when I turned over the goblet, it leaked.

As the audience laughed, Johnny began to take off.

"Very impressive, Ed," he said. "You think the wine needs to breathe a little more? Or are you auditioning for a jamboree of the Laguna Elks? What other things can you not wrap with that stuff? Is that the stuff the CIA uses for leaks?"

And now my instinct took over, the instinct that had moved me to cut off Johnny's tie and slap his face and set fire to his misfiring jokes. With the wine, the glass, and the wrap, I went around to the front of Johnny's desk. I had to prove that the wrap worked. Of course, at moments like this, it would have been fair to wonder how much longer *I* would work.

Summoning my courage, I filled the glass with wine, put on the wrap with the greatest care, and turned it upside down over Johnny's head. In a miracle fit for the Bible, nothing leaked.

"Ed," Johnny said, "the next time I have to wrap inverted glasses of wine, that's the stuff for me."

twenty-eight

The Magic Behind the Magic

Johnny the young magician, the Great Carsoni, had used his talent to prepare himself before dazzling America with his much bigger one. He had the same routine before every show. About ten minutes before our taping began, I would see him rolling a quarter or half-dollar along his fingers or flipping cards. This was a man so passionate about magic that one night when he was ten years old, he asked his mother to pick a card, and she had to reach up for it from the tub where she was taking a bath.

And from time to time, he was a human ashtray. He would put a cigarette butt in one of his hands, and then, moments later, five butts would appear in the other.

This magician's routine was how Johnny both relaxed and focused himself for the magic to come. While his mind prepared for the show, his hands were always in action, filling every minute with some kind of activity. If it wasn't magic, it was drumming with two pencils on a legal pad.

And he always prepared alone. Many stars have entourages that include secretaries, hairdressers, gofers, masseurs, tennis pros, and proctologists. Johnny did it all alone. As I once said, he packed a tight suitcase. About ten years after I said this, Johnny asked me, "What did you mean, I pack a tight suitcase?" He had been brooding about the thought for all that time. How's *that* for a long take!

What I had meant, of course, was that he was not a man of excess. The way he traveled—taking only the things he needed—was the style of his whole life. He always traveled light, always carrying his own bag, sometimes through airports where people kept showing how clever they were by telling him the words he had heard ten thousand times: *"I'm naked in front of you every night and my husband never minds . . . You're the funniest man I've ever been to bed with . . . I'm always in bed with you, and it's ruining my sex life."*

In playing *The Tonight Show* or a live date on the road, Johnny would arrive alone, do the job, and then leave, never with any fanfare or any kind of ceremony.

"My success just evolved from working hard at the business at hand every day," he said in an interview. "Talent alone won't make you a success or being in the right place at the right time. The most important question is, Are you ready?"

But Johnny wasn't ready for his final exit. In all our conversations, he never talked about his funeral. Like me and all other intelligent people, he planned to be immortal. However, just in case immortality didn't work out for him, he told me that he wanted a private departure.

And so, the final resting place of his ashes is known only to Alexis and his family.

No ceremony. That was the key. Johnny had a trim and frugal style, a low-key style typical of a man from Nebraska. He wanted attention only for one hour every night, but no fuss about him before or after he had done his job and gone home. That's how I feel about Johnny's entire life. He came without fanfare, got the job done, and then left.

By frugal, I certainly do not mean a lack of generosity. Johnny gave my youngest child, Katherine Mary, a sterling silver frame with her name on it. He gave me the most expensive watch I have ever owned, with the inscription, "Don't look up, Mrs. Thompson." He gave millions to the University of Nebraska and public schools

Courtesy of Stephen Cox Collection

Two blue suits with Doc Severinsen, who was probably preparing to play Joseph in his coat of many colors.

in his hometown. And he made large donations to organizations you probably never heard of, like Children of the Night, which cares for young prostitutes. Like Frank Sinatra, Johnny made all his contributions secretly because, like any man from Nebraska, he wanted no fuss made about them.

Johnny's frugality was his loathing of extravagance and the ornate.

"I don't need millions," he once told me. "I don't need eight houses or eighty-eight cars or three hundred suits. How many houses can you live in? How many suits can you wear? How many meals a day can you eat?"

Five or six would have been fine for me.

Johnny with Angie Dickinson and felow magician Orson Welles, who was never able to make his troubles disappear.

Getty Images

Johnny's ego was as self-assured as any I have ever known. "I have an ego like everyone else," he once told me, "but I don't need it to be stroked."

His head was never swelled by the success of *The Tonight Show,* even though he knew that the show was so appealing that it was "more effective than birth control pills."

Johnny's control of his ego, his blend of perspective and humility, allowed him to shine the brightest light on other comedians, especially when they were unknown. It was his nature to always make his guests look their best. Johnny liked any good young comedian who was just starting out because he knew the feeling of early struggle. He never forgot doing his own stand-up comedy in a small room in Bakersfield; and even a *big* room in Bakersfield qualified as the Pacific pits.

Show Business Superstition

In 1991, Johnny's annual salary was twenty million dollars, the highest in the history of television, but he didn't use it for three hundred suits. Even though he had his own line of clothing, I thought he might have needed to change his cuff links to a pair that didn't suggest Halloween.

One day in his dressing room before the show, I happened to look at his French cuffs and saw two different cuff links.

"I know you're always in the forefront of style," I said, "so I guess two different cuff links is the latest cool fashion and I'll start doing it. Is there anything else I should start doing? Like wearing my shorts inside out?"

"Ed," he said, "you could get a kidney transplant from Ralph Lauren and you'd still be as cool as Barney Fife. Two different cuff links isn't part of my clothing line; it's an old show business superstition."

"From a Latvian telethon, right?"

twenty-nine

At Least Tonto Didn't Have to Keep Laughing

Of all the twenty-two thousand guests that Johnny had, the one with whom I most identified was Jay Silverheels, the Native American actor who played Tonto on *The Lone Ranger*. Of course, he never went out drinking with the Lone Ranger, but he might have played the drums. And in talking to Johnny, I never sounded like Cookie Monster. In those pre-PC days, Tonto did a lot of grunting. The only word he spoke that had more than one syllable was *Kimosabe*.

"So you were the Lone Ranger's closest buddy for all those years," said Johnny. "Sort of Ed with feathers. No, actually, Four Feathers were with Ed a lot."

"Yes, I hung out with him," said Jay Silverheels, "even though he was the stuffiest guy west of Newark. Man, did he take himself seriously!"

"He wasn't a lot of laughs, was he?" said Johnny.

"You got that right."

"And he kept sending you to town to get supplies. Why didn't he ever go himself?"

"Maybe he thought the people in town didn't like him. But *I* was the only one who didn't like him. He never heard of the Emancipation Proclamation."

"Yes, news traveled kinda slow out West."

"And I washed his clothes and ironed his clothes and had to use all the damn bleach to keep his stuff so white. Twenty-five lousy years."

"And he always wore that mask?"

"He did."

"Tell me, did you ever get a look at his face?"

"Once. He let me peek under the mask."

"And?"

"No big deal."

"I think he saw too many *Zorro* films."

The Homework School of the Air

One of the most painful gags I can remember happened one night when we were doing the Homework School of the Air, which will never make the Comedy Hall of Fame, especially because there isn't one. The star of the Homework School of the Air was, of course, Johnny, although on this particular night he probably wished it had been his worst enemy.

"And now," I said, "a man who hasn't let education go to his head, the dean and entire faculty of the Homework School of the Air, Professor John W. Carson."

Don't ask me why we thought Professor John W. Carson was funny. And don't ask me anything else about the bit.

At any rate, out came Johnny in a cap and gown—his first mistake of the night.

"Professor," I said, "our first question is from a woman in East St. Louis."

"Why doesn't she move to West St. Louis?" asked Johnny. "That's the good side."

"And let's see if we can find the good side of this bit," I said.

Courtesy of Stephen Cox Collection

Skitch Henderson, Johnny, and me posing for the NBC calendar cover shortly after we started on *The Tonight Show.* The calendar was given to station affiliates, employees, and other friends of NBC.

"This woman would like to know, What is the most gullible animal?"

"What is the most gullible animal?" he asked, stalling for time until our flak jackets arrived.

"Yes," I said, "I'm not changing the question."

"The most gullible animal is the African mattayou."

"What's a mattayou?" I said.

"Nothing. What's a matta you?"

The audience groaned. Kernels of corn should have fallen on us both.

"This audience would scalp tickets to a cockfight," said Johnny, again the master of the rescue.

We should have mercifully ended the sketch right there, but something—stupidity, perhaps—moved us to show there were no depths to which we would not sink.

"You probably don't know that I'm a music teacher," said Professor Johnny.

"Is that germane?" I asked.

"Some of it is germane and some is Austrian. In fact, I'm tutoring a young lady in Austrian composers."

"Mahler?" I said.

"Every chance I get."

The audience topped its previous groan.

Moments later, during the commercial break, Johnny said to me, "We better not do stuff like that on the air."

It was hard to remember that the man who had dropped those bombs was a perfectionist. On this forgettable night, the perfectionist must have been hoping for a tape delay—of a couple of years.

Jackie Revere

Johnny probably wanted a long tape delay on another night when a sketch was just as painful. Late in 1975, the Mighty Carson Art Players decided to either celebrate or desecrate America's Bicentennial. In a sketch called "America's First Comedian," Johnny came out as a colonial stand-up comic, Jackie Revere. Well, it quickly turned out that *Paul* Revere had gotten more laughs when he cried, "The British are coming!"

"I rode my wife halfway to Lexington until I found out I was on the wrong nag," Jackie Revere said, and there was respectful silence. "You know how I got the title Minuteman? On my honeymoon."

There was continued silence from people who had first heard that joke in nursery school.

"But I'm surprised I hung around that long," said Jackie Revere with the guts of Paul. "My wife is so ugly that she won a King George look-alike contest."

Johnny was being as funny as King George.

Okay, Johnny, I thought, *it's another 911 call for you.*

Hearing the call, he answered it by turning to the audience with a lingering look of puzzled innocence, a look that said, *It's not my fault; maybe it's yours.*

It was a look that would have made Jack Benny know that his legacy bloomed in Burbank. I wanted to help Johnny with the rescue, but there was no way I could get into the sketch because the entire solemn event was in costume. Finally, however, I got a cue.

"Philadelphia is so small," said Jackie Revere, "that town drunk is an elective office."

"Did someone mention my civic position?" I said. "Mr. Gordon ran my campaign for the job."

"Ed, come on in and go down with us," said Johnny. "Come and salute the *Titanic*."

I don't remember how we did it, but at last, as Johnny and I had done so often before, we became comic firemen who somehow managed to pull some laughs from the ashes.

Of course, like all entertainers who go before the public day after day, Johnny struggled with a maddening problem: he was competing with himself, and the better each show was, the harder it was to follow it with one just as good.

"There's only one solution," Johnny told me. "We have to be rotten from time to time to make our next ones look good."

I never liked it when people told me, "The show was okay, but Tuesday's was better."

"Okay, we'll stink tomorrow," I wanted to say, "and then you can catch our comeback on Friday."

Our opportunity for a comeback was never more inviting than after one Homework School of the Air that actually stopped the show, but not for the traditional reason. It stopped the show when Johnny discovered that my index cards with the questions didn't match the answers he was getting from the cue cards behind the camera. Of course, this lack of synchronization could not have hurt a sketch that brought to mind a living will. In fact, giving answers to wrong questions might have been funnier than giving wrong answers to the questions that matched. Gum surgery also might have been funnier.

This sketch had been going down the drain when Johnny suddenly grabbed the index cards from my hand and began to look for a certain one that he felt had to be there. As he did so, I sat there in naked splendor, waiting for Johnny to save the moment with his wit. But for the first time I could ever remember, his wit was silent. He just kept going through the cards while I began wondering if this might be a good time to lie down in my dressing room. And it might have been if I'd *had* a dressing room.

This is the first dead air we've ever had on the show, I thought. *And Johnny can't resuscitate it because he's busy doing research.*

At last, however, he surfaced and said to the audience, "Ed may not quite be on top of what's going on here. He just dropped in to get his mail between *Star Search* and his blooper show."

This particular sketch wasn't *good* enough for the blooper show.

Because Johnny was the best rebounder in the history of television, the show needed these lows to inspire his highs. He had another wonderful chance to bounce back after he had spoofed a Ronald Reagan press conference with a sketch that was almost good enough for a Rotary roast. Sometimes *The Tonight Show*'s writers were on target, but other times, it seemed that they deliberately wanted to challenge Johnny's powers of recovery by giving him material that belonged in intensive care.

"Mr. President," asked a reporter, "what is the state of our relations with China?"

"Well," said Johnny as Reagan, "you know what happens: you have a peace talk with China and two hours later you're at war again."

Nothing could have been more challenging for Johnny than having to tell an ancient joke *wrong*. If you *had* to retell it, and I can think of no reason why, the retelling *should* have been "two hours later, you have to talk peace again."

The writer who had descended to that subterranean level should have been sent directly to China—on a slow boat. I cringe remembering a few other lines.

"Mr. President," asked the reporter, "have you any new appointments?"

"Yes," said Johnny, "to see my barber at three o'clock."

"And what came out of the last joint session of Congress?"

"We all got stoned."

No proof of Johnny's talent was more dramatic than his ability to somehow manage to get laughs during and right after material that would not have disturbed Yom Kippur or Lent.

thirty

Rowan and Carson's Laugh-In

Dave Garroway and Jack Paar could sell good and bad books. Arthur Godfrey could sell mediocre singers, soap powder, and tea. But Johnny achieved a power that American television never had seen. He was able to sell toilet paper when it wasn't even a sponsor.

One December night in 1973, Johnny said in his monologue, "You know what's disappearing from the supermarket shelves? Toilet paper. No, I'm not kidding. There's an acute shortage of toilet paper in the United States."

Because *The Tonight Show* had no fact-checker, this bit of news had all the veracity of the *Saddam Hussein Report.* Nevertheless, the next morning, many of Johnny's twelve million viewers ran out and bought all the toilet paper they could find. By noon, most of the stores were out of it and no one wanted to hear Johnny say, "Let me talk to you about diarrhea."

"It's a ridiculous panic," Johnny told me, "but I've got to stop it."

"Yes," I said, "the country has the runs."

"Save the doo-doo jokes for Mel Brooks," he said. "This is serious. I didn't know we had so many people who believed what I said."

"I never thought more than a handful."

"This is nonsense, but it's serious."

"You're right, of course," I said. "I checked with Tom Brokaw, and there definitely is no shortage."

"No, just a shortage of brains," he said. "Mine."

On the next show, Johnny apologized for scaring America and said there was no shortage of toilet paper. His viewers, however, must have thought that El Moldo was talking because the stampede to the stores continued. It ended in a couple of weeks, after both Johnny and I had learned the awesome power he had.

"Look at the bright side," I told him. "You didn't say there was a shortage of Gordon's."

He looked at me with that inimitable smile.

"Too soon."

Johnny had the power to move not just toilet paper but also products that belonged in a garage sale. On one particular show, I gave a demonstration of a new model of a certain brand of tape recorder. After Johnny had said a nursery rhyme into the microphone, I smilingly hit the playback button and there was silence.

"Many times you have had that," I told Carnac, but a sponsor wasn't paying for this to be one of them.

"Oh well," Johnny said, "Edison didn't always get it right the first time either. But this recorder *looks* good and it probably has a shot at working sometimes."

"Edison is near Linden," I said.

"Maybe little Gordon can get it to work," said my smooth pickup man.

In spite of this dramatic failure seen by millions, on the following day, the sales of this particular tape recorder jumped. In other words, we had sold a defective product, like a clock whose hands didn't move. It was a sales jump that made no sense, but I finally figured it out. In thirty years of sketches, Johnny also had made no sense but had left America entranced. And now the people in that trance were doing anything he asked them to do. It was his greatest feat of magic.

I once had wondered: *Is there* nothing *this man can't do?* The producer of *Laugh-In*, George Schlatter, must have wondered the same thing on the day that Dick Martin, one of *Laugh-In*'s co-stars, didn't show up for the taping at the studio just down the hall from Johnny's. Quickly, George walked the few yards to Johnny's office.

"Johnny," he asked, "could you come down the hall for a second? I need a little help today."

"Sure," said Johnny, who was always willing to do anything for someone he liked, "but if this is another one of Ed's surprise parties, I'm replacing him with someone from the Connecticut School of Broadcasting."

"Just come with me!"

After George had led Johnny into the *Laugh-In* studio, he said, "Johnny, here's what I need. Would you please stand right there and on cue read the cards?"

"George, you want me to—"

Suddenly, an announcer said, "Ladies and gentlemen, here are Dan Rowan and Dick Martin!"

And Johnny then did what George has told me was the best impression of Dick Martin ever done. Of course, I wasn't surprised. I know that Johnny could have done Goldie Hawn too.

A Genuine Listener

Johnny's brilliant imitation of Dick Martin makes me think of the punch line of one of his birthday jokes that sums up the marvel that Johnny was: *"That's just the tip of the iceberg."*

Americans never knew that Johnny was an iceberg himself, *not* the temperature of his disposition but the visibility of his talent. Only half of it was on view. Johnny played the guitar well, but never on the show; he was a fine ventriloquist, but never on the show; he was an excellent drummer, but never on the show; and his supreme mastery of interviewing was probably unappreciated by most of his audience.

Johnny was a better listener than a federal agent with earphones. In every talk with a guest, he intelligently played off the guest's last comment, always aware that his next question was in the last answer. Many TV hosts don't listen because they're busy thinking of their next non sequitur.

"How are you?" the host asks.

"Suicidally depressed," the guest replies.

"Glad to hear it! And how are the wife and kids?"

"My wife ran off with a UPS man and all the kids have scurvy."

"Great! What are your plans now?"

"I'm entering a monastery in Kenya, but only one with rehab."

"That's terrific. Are you married?"

"Still married to the woman I just told you about, even though she left me."

"Wish we had time to hear your recipe for marital happiness. What do you consider your best film?"

"An X-ray of my molars."

"Yes, I loved that one too. Tell me, was there much tension on the set?"

Associated Press, AP

Mark Twain said that the difference between the right words and almost the right words is the difference between lightning and a lightning bug. As Johnny works on his opening monologue in his New York office in 1963, lightning is about to flash.

Johnny, however, was genuinely curious, listened carefully to every word said to him, and then moved in precisely the right direction. He was a remarkable blend of amused observer and participant too, one of the few hosts who actually read the books of writers who came to the show. In fact, his talks with guests were so good that I had to change my own preparation for the show.

Early in the New York run, I always read the notes about the guests so that I might have my own ideas for questions. In about the fourth year of the show, however, I realized that Johnny was never using his notes for questions, but always responding spontaneously. My studying the notes was like my preparing for an exam in improvisation.

Johnny never talked to his guests before the show or during the commercial breaks because he didn't want them saying something that belonged on the air. He would talk only to me during breaks.

"Johnny didn't like me," a guest would sometimes tell me after the show.

"Why do you say that?" I would ask.

"Because he didn't talk to me during the breaks."

"He never talks to anyone but me during the breaks," I said with renewed respect for the man who knew when silence was golden.

thirty-one

Two Bawdy Buddies for Buddy Rich

Buddy Rich was the world's best drummer and an inspiration for the world's 3,957th best drummer, Johnny Carson. Johnny, who loved Buddy as both an artist and a friend, was dismayed to learn one day during the New York run of *The Tonight Show* that Buddy lay gravely ill in a Philadelphia hospital. I don't remember his particular illness, but I do remember the doctors feared that he might not make it. And Buddy feared something worse than dying—that he would never play the drums again. With his legs in pulleys, he was deeply depressed, for drummers use their legs as well as their hands. Buddy had been a tap dancer, a talent that enriched his artistry with the double bass drums.

A friend of mine, a big-band booker named Willard Alexander, told me of Buddy's sad state and then said, "Ed, I'm going to make a strange request. Buddy is as down as a man can be. Would you and Johnny consider coming down to visit him? And the sooner, the better."

"Willard," I said, "let me ask Johnny right away. You know his feelings for Buddy."

When I told Johnny about Buddy's plight, he said, "I know just what we'll do for him: a bawdy Carnac!"

The next day after taping the show, Johnny and I drove to Philadelphia and went to Jefferson Hospital. At about nine o'clock, the people at the hospital saw a man entering in a flowing robe and a turban that belonged on a sheik with a bigger head. Was this a head case that belonged at a different hospital? Buddy's doctors had given us permission to try to save his life with an old miracle drug called laughter.

Minutes later, with Johnny waiting in the fourth floor hall, I walked into Buddy's room, where a doctor was standing at a heart monitor.

"And here he is," I boomed. "That mysterious visitor from the East who long ago went south . . . the man Nostradamus predicted would need something more than Nodoz . . . a man too strange even for Philadelphia . . . Carnac the Magnificent!"

And into the room came Johnny while Buddy's ropes began to dance from his laughter.

"Stop!" he cried. "You're killing me!"

"Many have wanted to kill Carnac," I said. "Especially the mother and the father he never had."

While Buddy howled, I turned to Carnac, held up an envelope, and said, "O, Endlessly Nondescript One, here is your first answer."

Johnny took the envelope, read it, and said, "Coitus interruptus."

"Coitus interruptus," I said.

"Carnac finds such repetition a pain in the ass," said Johnny.

"Pain in the ass," I said.

And then, he opened the envelope and read the question: "Which Roman emperor had the shortest reign?"

While Buddy tried to keep himself from falling out of bed, I gave Johnny another envelope, which he held up and read, "Blue balls."

"Blue balls," I said.

"That's just what I said, O Large Loon of the West," said Johnny, who then read the question: "What are melancholy cotillions?"

"And your third envelope, O Blessed One," I said, handing it to him.

"Dry hump," said Johnny.

Johnny was America's greatest late-night entertainer, who also played drums. Buddy Rich was America's greatest drummer, who also stayed up late. They had a deep affection for each other.

"Dry hump," I said.

"You can be replaced by a lamppost," said Johnny, who then read the question. "What does a camel do after a bath?"

Into the room now came a young doctor who hadn't been briefed about our act. "What's all the screaming in here?" he asked. "Oh—Johnny Carson!"

"Won't you join us, Doctor?" said Johnny. "We're having more laughs than your last operation."

"I love your show," the doctor said, who then turned to me and cried, "Hi-yooo!"

"That was *Snow White and the Seven Dwarfs*," said Johnny. "Ed auditioned, but he didn't make the height. Carnac do one more question and then go play with the nurses."

"Carnac sounding like Tonto," I said. "Maybe in wrong sketch."

"No, wrong hospital. Need neurological one."

"Your final answer," I said, handing him the envelope.

Holding it up, Johnny said, "A Frenchman with crabs."

"A Frenchman with crabs," I said.

"And may they visit you—not the French, the other," said Johnny, who opened the envelope and read, "What is Jacques Itch?"

Walking over to the bouncing Buddy, Johnny turned to the young doctor and said, "Doctor, let me explain that to you. This man is a musician, and so he knows very few words in English—in fact, in any language. Jacques is a play on . . ."

After laughing so hard that he almost slipped his pulleys, Buddy went on to a recovery that left his doctors incredulous. Johnny and I had taken alternative medicine about as far as it could go.

thirty-two

Gone with the Wand

Once, during the last commercial, Johnny turned to me and casually asked, "So do you think we should do another year?"

"Oh, absolutely," I said.

"Okay, I'll tell them tomorrow."

Years later, however, Johnny's atomic bomb wasn't dropped for me ahead of time. He didn't tell me during a commercial that he was leaving the show. Like everyone else on the staff, I heard this stunning news when he announced it at a meeting of NBC affiliates in 1991. And I felt like John O'Hara, who, when told of the death of George Gershwin, said, "I don't have to believe it if I don't want to."

So many people watched *The Tonight Show* that in 1991 Johnny was responsible for making sixty million dollars for NBC, 15 percent of its annual revenue. By that time, NBC had become a division of General Electric.

"GE just gave me the greatest honor of my life," Johnny said on his final show. "They named me Employee of the Month. God knows, that was a dream come true."

No television performer arriving today could ever have the impact of Johnny Carson for two reasons. First, there will never again be a show with the power of *The Tonight Show*, which moved millions of people to say at watercoolers the following morning, "Did you see Carson last night?" Today, a hundred cable channels are cluttered with round-the-clock stand-up comics who compete to see who is the most mind-numbing. If you walk through the wrong cellar door to deliver a pizza, you can find yourself doing fifteen minutes of material that at its peak is unfunny and at its depth something to chill the soul.

Courtesy of Stephen Cox Collection

"Johnny, I don't care how big a star you are. This is supposed to be black tie."

The bigger reason no one could ever again have Johnny's impact is that no one would ever pay the dues that he paid. Johnny was a comedian, magician, ventriloquist, writer, interviewer, and musician. He had honed all those talents not just in small clubs in Bakersfield but in places that made Bakersfield seem like Times Square. In the very beginning, Johnny's stage had been the back of a chicken truck on the dirt roads of rural Nebraska, where his magic was preceded not by Ed McMahon but by the crow of a rooster. Johnny had walked through not curtains but chicken feed, hardly a harbinger for the man who one day would be the highest paid performer in television history.

But a little hay was always in his hair, for Johnny was a comedian who blended Manhattan, Kansas, with Manhattan, New York. He was a man who let Aunt Blabby talk about Nietzsche, even if she thought Nietzsche was a laxative. Johnny was a man who glided smoothly between the broad and the subtle. One night, however, he tested the intelligence of the viewers in both Manhattans.

Fencing with Words

Johnny's guest that night was Charles Grodin, an actor who was either fey or weird, depending on your feeling for him. Grodin had come to *The Tonight Show* to promote a book about himself that sold for twenty-five dollars.

"That's a lot of money for a book, especially one about you," said Johnny. "People who aren't interested in you—and there must be millions—would be more likely to buy it for ten or fifteen bucks. After all, this isn't a life of Lincoln. Or even Ivana Trump."

Suddenly, Grodin, who sometimes seemed to be commuting from another planet, said, "You don't really care about the book. You don't really care about *anything*." Grodin's tone was so tongue-in-cheek that it became foot-in-mouth.

"You're right, I don't," said Johnny, seasoning his humor with pique. "I don't care about the book or about you either. I'm just looking for warm bodies to fill an hour. I'd take a chipmunk in heat. I'd take a chimpanzee with flu."

It was a moment that left me uneasy. Johnny, both joking and angry, had been forced to defend himself with absurd words, a sardonic admission that the man who listened to guests more thoughtfully than any humorist in the history of TV was just looking for mammals that had a pulse. Grodin had missed the irony of Johnny connecting with him well enough to slice him up like Zorro.

"*Zorro, Ed?*" Johnny is saying now. *"More like Zeppo. Or Harpo, maybe."*

"I just meant, Johnny, that you were brilliant at oral fencing."

"Oral fencing? You mean orthodontia?"

"Yes, Johnny, day and night, I keep hearing lines like that . . . and seeing . . . and remembering . . . Remember the man who played the nose flute?"

"Of course. I wanted him to blow a concerto."

"Or at least sneeze a good chord."

"You think he played by ear?"

"Why is that funny from you but painful from anyone else?"

"Precisely the words for a clown who's moonlighting as a proctologist."

"Remember the night you barged into Rickles's studio because he'd broken your cigarette box?"

"I was too dumb to realize he had done me a favor."

Courtesy of Stephen Cox Collection

The multicolored curtain became almost as famous as the NBC peacock.

"And remember when you took a bath?"

"Yes, every other night in the monologue."

"Hardly, my friend."

"Still my faithful Indian companion."

"Even Tonto could have told you why the monologue was so good: you always knew exactly what the country was thinking."

"Right: Poland."

"Remember the night you did the monologue lying in a bed because that was the way everyone watched you?"

"Yes, my switch. I wanted all the people in bed to stand up."

"And salute that Roman emperor Coitus Interruptus."

"You know, Ed, I always wondered how many people made love while still watching me. And how many guys said to women, 'Was it good for

you?' And how many women said, 'Well, the monologue was better last night.'"

In the years after he left the show, Johnny was a happy man. He was married to a woman he adored, he loved playing tennis on his own court, to which he walked through a tunnel that ran from his house under a highway; and he loved his yacht, the 130-foot *Serengeti.* If you have a happy marriage, a tennis court, and a yacht, what else do you need?

Not to get sticky about it, but number one on the list is really enough, and that was Johnny's Alexis, the stunning woman who first caught his eye when she walked past him on the beach at Malibu. She was wearing a bikini and carrying an empty wineglass.

He and I had the same values, though not the same valuables. I also had a yacht, but next to Johnny's, mine would have looked like a dinghy.

The last time I saw Johnny, about a year before he died, he *looked* like a million dollars. On the *Serengeti,* we had chicken, a couple of glasses of red wine, and then we just sat there and reminisced, going back and forth the way we did on the show. We talked about our kids and our careers and the state of America, just two lucky guys who loved each other and the good luck they had found together.

When I walked down the gangplank, I turned and gave him a salute and he gave one to me. Mine was a little better because a Marine colonel usually gives a smarter salute than a Navy ensign, especially when the colonel is thanking the ensign for his career. I would have given Johnny that same salute if his rank had been Gomer Pyle's.

thirty-three

Too Soon

Of all that I keep remembering, no moment was sweeter than the night that Elizabeth Taylor turned Johnny into her straight man.

On the show that night, Johnny and Elizabeth were discussing astrology.

"What's your sign?" he asked her.

"I'm a Pisces," Elizabeth replied.

"I married a Pisces," he said.

"I'm sure you did," said she.

When Johnny stopped laughing, he asked, "Any new project you want to talk about?"

"No, an old project," Elizabeth said. "You. I just want to thank you for so many years of marvelous entertainment."

Well, Johnny, that's it. Too soon. For you, *many years too soon. It's just not fair. Of course, as you once said, "If life were fair, Elvis would be alive and all the impersonators would be dead."*

You think little Gordon would like this book? I would trade him and every other reader for—"Two grown men. Graduates of major universities."

I wish you could be playing the drums behind me now, as you did at Jilly's and Danny's and Sneaky Pete's, while I sing this one last song.

Thanks for the memories
Of thirty years of gags,
Of funny bits

Courtesy of Stephen Cox Collection

The team that put *The Tonight Show* together for many years was Doc Severinsen, Johnny, myself, and, in the back, our director, Bobby Quinn, and producer, Fred de Cordova.

(Well, some the pits)
Like ties turned into rags
How mellow we were.

Thanks for the memories
Of flying high with you,
While down our legs
Ran uncooked eggs.
Two grown men full of goo;
How yellow we were.

Thanks for the memories.
Banana number two
Loved everything
That you would wing
When headed for deep doo.
Cool fellow you were.

Thanks for the memories.
Aunt Blabby and the rest.
And Carol Wayne
With outline plain;
Her top was your hope chest.
Like Jell-O they were.

Never were we ever parted,
Until you left me brokenhearted.
What golden years!
Four thousand "Heeeeere's"

So thanks for the memories.
It all was one sweet dream.
So much applause
For one whose drawers
Once filled up with whipped cream.

Thanks for the memories.
Remember Tiny Tim?
When he was wed,
I think you said,
"The gown should be on him."

Thanks for the memories
Of wine and roses days.
Well, roses no.
The other, though,
Became our Linden phase.

Thanks for the memories.
You always were the best.
You were the star
Who packed my car
With clues for my arrest.

Thanks for the memories.
Our days were one long lark.
So many games,
Some bright with flames;
I felt like Joan of Arc.

Yes, thanks for the memories
Of all those comic scats.
You brought me in,
I could have been
Out selling food for cats.
We showed ourselves
To be two elves.
No, overage rug rats.

Hi-yooo, my dear friend!

NBC/Globe Photos, Inc.